What Others are Saying
About the Author's Work

McConkey deserves to be applauded for writing the first Canadian solution-focused textbook. If your goal this year is to be a more effective teacher, principal or counsellor and you read only one work-related book, choose "Solving School Problems".

> Ronald Warner, Ph.D., Adjunct Professor, and Program Director of the Certificate Program in Solution-Focused Counselling, Faculty of Social Work, University of Toronto.

Nancy McConkey is an inspired presenter. She lives the solution-focused model.

> Fred Reekie, Ph.D., Associate Professor, Department of Educational Psychology and Special Education, University of Saskatchewan

One of the top five workshops I have attended in the last ten years. Nancy ranks with the well-known names in solution-focused counselling.

> Pat Heuchert, Counsellor, Manitoba Teachers' Society

The solution-focused approach has made a big difference in our school.

> Del Bouck, B.R.E., B.Ed., M.Ed. School Principal, Alberta

This is the one of the most useful workshops I have attended in 27 years of teaching.

> Barry Pratte, Teacher, Alberta

I don't think you can go back to problem-oriented thinking once you have taken this course. This workshop accelerates the creation of new ideas and helps me work with very difficult situations.

Paul Bohn, Family Support Worker,
British Columbia

I wanted to let you know how beneficial the Solution-Focused Workshop has been for me as a school principal. When I returned to school on Wednesday, I had the opportunity to use the ideas with an upset parent, a problem student, a neglected child, and for myself as a parent. In all four cases, the tone of the meetings was very civilized and a great deal of information came forth in a short amount of time. I am excited to have received this information and would recommend it to others.

Gary Crossman, School Principal,
New Brunswick

Nancy did a two-day workshop for our school principals and counsellors. I received rave reviews from the participants about the value of the workshop and her skills as a presenter. I will be having her back!

Margie Layden-Oreto, Director of Student Services,
New Brunswick

This is an outstanding book, full of case examples, and easy–to-use strategies that will help professionals solve school problems more quickly.

Maureen Leahey, R.N., Ph.D., Director, Family Therapy
Training Program, Calgary Health Region

Solving School Problems

About the Author

Nancy McConkey, MSW, is a family therapist, professional speaker and leading expert in the solution-focused approach. Informative and dynamic, Nancy has presented hundreds of workshops to professionals from schools, hospitals, psychiatric facilities, community health clinics, child welfare agencies, substance abuse treatment centres, and mental health agencies. She is a sought after keynote speaker, both nationally and internationally, for education, health care and counselling conferences.

Nancy is an Approved Supervisor and Clinical Member of the American Association for Marriage and Family Therapy (AAMFT); an Adjunct Faculty Member, Family Therapy Training Program, Calgary Health Region; a Registered Social Worker, Alberta Association of Social Workers; and a Professional Member, Canadian Association of Professional Speakers (CAPS).

Nancy McConkey can be reached at 403-216-TALK (8255) or www. solutiontalk.ab.ca.

Solving School Problems

Solution-Focused Strategies for Principals, Teachers, and Counsellors

Nancy McConkey

Alberta, Canada

National Library of Canada Cataloguing in Publication

McConkey, Nancy, 1952-
    Solving school problems : solution-focused strategies for
principals, teachers, and counsellors / Nancy McConkey.

Includes bibliographical references and index.
ISBN 0-9689472-0-4

    1. Problem children—Education. 2. Teacher-student relationships.
3. Solution-focused therapy. 4. Counseling in elementary education.
5. Counseling in secondary education. I. Title.

LC4801.5.M33 2002   371.4'6   C2002-902808-6

The author and publisher have done everything possible to make this book
accurate, up to date, and in accordance with accepted standards professional
standards at the time of publication. The author, editor, and publisher make
no warranty, express or implied, in regards to the contents of this book. Any
practice described in this book should always be applied in accordance with
the appropriate professional code of conduct that governs the practitioner,
and with the appropriate standard of care.

Published by: Solution Talk Press

Box 247, Bragg Creek, Alberta, Canada, T0L 0K0
Website: www.solutiontalk.ab.ca
Email: soltalk@telusplanet.net
Ph: 1-866-30-4TALK (8255) or 403-216-8255

Attention: Organizations and Schools. Quantity discounts of this book are available.
For information about this book, workshops on this topic, and future resources,
please refer to the order form in the back of this book.

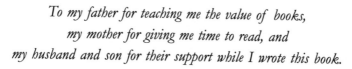

*To my father for teaching me the value of books,
my mother for giving me time to read, and
my husband and son for their support while I wrote this book.*

Contents

Part One
Overview

Part Two
Key Components

Part Three
Facing Tough Problems

Foreword

For a long time I have believed that educators need a new way of thinking about student management. Initially, I experimented with traditional discipline strategies that focused on students' problems. In search of a fresh approach, as a teaching team, we wanted a student management system that did not make discipline the focus of our school. Instead, the system had to enhance our school's instructional focus on student achievement. Our desire was to implement an approach that would be life changing, forward thinking and consistent across the board for administrators, teachers, counsellors, support staff members and most importantly, the students. Our search led us to adopt the solution-focused model.

All our teaching team members have received training with Nancy McConkey, in the solution-focused approach. It has been my experience that these skills have helped us make the paradigm shift from focusing on the problem itself to creating solutions that make lasting change happen. The experience has been positive for all parties involved and has naturally allowed ownership of the problem to be placed where it belongs. It has provided equilibrium for staff members – alleviating their frustration with traditional discipline methods and the infamous belief that discipline was a "vicious cycle." Solution-focused strategies will help you with your discipline problems – the problems encountered in every grade.

Nancy McConkey's motivational methods encouraged and assisted our professionals to develop their shared leadership skills. It has been my personal experience that solution-focused strategies not only enhance student-teacher relationships but also provide a way for teachers and support staff members to support one another in a collaborative manner.

This book provides a wealth of "hands on" skills that will allow you to affect your school environment immediately. As George Bernard Shaw so aptly stated, "Imagination is the beginning of creation. You imagine what you desire, you will what you imagine, and at last you create what you will." As you read through these pages, I encourage you to put all biases aside and allow yourself to envision what your school might look like if the *"Solution Miracle"* were to take place.

Del Bouck, B.R.E., B.Ed., M.Ed.
Principal,
Edmonton Public Schools

Preface

I have been conducting workshops on the solution-focused approach for over fifteen years, from coast to coast. The positive feedback I have received from school principals, counsellors and teachers over these years has been inspiring. Education professionals tell me regularly how useful the solution-focused model has been in their work with students and parents.

Over the years, workshop participants have asked me for more specific information on how to use the solution-focused model with school problems. They wanted a book that was practical, non-academic, and easy to read. So, with those specific requests in mind, I was inspired to write.

Although there are other books on the subject, what was missing in the marketplace was a clear and practical guidebook for school professionals. What was needed was a book that "modeled" solution-focused skills. To that end, I have included a generous number of case studies on a wide range of behaviour management issues. Also, I have included many samples of questions, techniques, and strategies that can be used in a wide variety of situations.

I hope you find these inclusions make the book practical and the ideas easy to apply. This book can function as a companion piece for my seminars or on its own as a teaching tool for anyone interested in becoming solution-focused. Whatever your role may be, it is my belief that the solution-focused model will help you in your work with students and parents.

Nancy McConkey

Acknowledgments

I would like to thank my friend and mentor, Dr. Maureen Leahey who has been a steady source of encouragement and advice. Also, I offer many thanks to Elaine Kuhlemeyer and Del Bouck. Both of them carefully reviewed the first draft and provided useful feedback. I am very grateful to my editor, Darla Rettie, who helped to make my dream come true.

The solution-focused model helped me to become more effective as a counsellor and I became passionately committed to learning it. I was fortunate to learn from some of the pioneers in this field. Particularly, I would like to acknowledge Steve de Shazer and Insoo Kim Berg. I spent a week at their center in Milwaukee and their writing and work continue to inspire me.

Over the years, the writings by Yvonne Dolan, Michael Durrant, Linda Metcalf, Scott Miller, Bill O'Hanlon, Matthew Selekman, Jane Peller, John Walter and Michelle Weiner-Davis have greatly influenced my practice.

Finally, I want to thank my counselling clients. I learned from each of them— it has been a privilege to be a part of their lives.

Part One
Overview

Introduction

A principal meets with a new grade eight student and her foster mother. The student has been transferred to his school for a "fresh start." Her academic average, at the end of her last semester, was ten percent. The principal wonders how he can help this student.

A high school counsellor talks with a student who is depressed. The counsellor has a high caseload and doesn't have time to do long-term counselling with students. She wonders how she can be more effective in the limited time that she has with the students she counsels.

An elementary school teacher struggles with how to help a young student who has been diagnosed with attention deficit disorder. Her usual strategies aren't working with him.

The above three scenarios reflect typical situations where intervention is called for. Over the course of the book, we will return to these scenarios. You will learn how the principal, teacher and counsellor used solution-focused strategies, in each of these situations, to help these students quickly and effectively.

Problems facing students and school professionals are increasingly complex. Time and financial resources for solving school problems are often hard to come by. The solution-focused model gives school professionals practical tools for solving problems with students and parents, rapidly and effectively. The model can be applied to a wide range of problems and with all age groups. When used by all school staff, the solution-focused approach can transform the entire school culture by creating a more cooperative, positive, strength-oriented atmosphere.

The solution-focused model is different from traditional problem-focused models. In the latter model, the emphasis is on the history of the problem, the causes of a problem, and on student deficits that need to be corrected. In contrast to this, the solution-focused model emphasizes times when the problem does *not* occur. These exceptions to the problem offer clues to solutions. The solution-focused model uses different types of questions to build on these exceptions and to elicit students' strengths, resources and ideas for change.

The solution-focused model also uses future-oriented questions to help students and parents to visualize a solution picture. Solution-focused questions and language help both the educators and the students to shift from problems to solutions. However, working in a solution-focused "style" involves more than just asking a few solution-focused questions. It is a step-by-step process, covered fully through the chapters of this book.

The three scenarios described at the beginning of this introduction come from actual case histories. These cases, and a selection of others, are used as teaching tools throughout the book. They bring the principles of the solution-focused model to life.

The key focus of this book is *how to* apply the skills that are discussed. In each case cited, you will learn *how* the principal, teacher or counsellor used solution-focused strategies to help the students and parents help themselves. By including a wealth of case transcripts, you will see how the theory holds up in real life situations!

Who Will Benefit From This Book

THIS BOOK IS WRITTEN FOR PRINCIPALS, school counsellors, teachers, special education teachers, guidance counsellors, behaviour strategists, behaviour adaptation teachers, family-school liaison workers and other professionals who work with school problems. It draws on my twenty years of experience as a family therapist working with children and their families as well as the hundreds of solution-focused workshops I have conducted for school professionals. Twenty-five case examples are presented[1] to help you learn how to use solution-focused language and questions.

A frequent request, from workshop participants, has been for a companion book to reinforce the content covered in my seminars. Educators wanted a book that was practical, non-academic, and easy to read. This book has been designed to stand alone as a teaching tool or to augment the material I cover in my solution-focused workshops. No matter what your role, the solution-focused model will help you in your work with students and parents.

Principals will learn how to

- defuse anger and resistance
- use solution-focused strategies for conflict resolution
- motivate students to change
- deal with bullying in a positive way
- use solution-focused discipline strategies
- facilitate solution-focused team building
- motivate staff members

Teachers will learn how to:

- handle difficult parent-teacher interviews
- resolve student conflicts quickly
- deal with students' anger management problems
- use brief, positive interventions in the classroom

---

[1] Names and other identifying facts have been changed to preserve confidentiality.

- work with difficult students
- motivate students to generate solutions
- develop solution-focused Individual Program Plans
- strengthen students' resiliency

Counsellors will learn how to:

- do single-session counselling
- use solution-focused techniques in groups
- do solution-focused assessments
- help students deal with Attention Deficit Disorder and other problems
- work quickly to promote change
- lead solution-focused meetings

Part One
Overview

Chapters One to Four give an overview of the solution-focused model. Chapter One examines how the solution-focused model differs from problem-focused models, and how it challenges traditional assumptions about school problems. This chapter describes the solution-building process and how to develop solution-focused questions. Chapter Two gives you ten guidelines for becoming solution-focused. Chapter Three describes how to use goal-setting questions with students and parents and how to shift a meeting from problem talk to solution talk. Chapter Four describes how to search for *islands of competence*, why it is important to focus on students' strengths, and how we can help to develop resilient children.

Part Two
Key Components

Chapters Five to Eight break the model down into key components and skills that you can immediately begin to use. Chapter Five demonstrates the use of scaling questions to create change, step by step. Chapter Six gives you clear instructions on how to structure a solution-focused meeting. Chapter Seven takes you into an actual interview, with a transcript of a solution-focused meeting. This will help you to see the entire solution-focused process in action. Chapter Eight describes how you can use solution-focused homework tasks with students and parents, to help them create and sustain change.

Part Three
Facing Tough Problems

Chapters Nine to Twelve focus on the tough problems that school professionals face. Strategies for working with difficult students are detailed in Chapter Nine. The focus is on two key issues: how to work with students who have been involuntarily sent for counselling, and what to do when a student blames others for her/his problems. Chapter Ten shows how principals can be solution-focused when disciplining students, dealing with bullying, and working with problem students. A case example shows how you can use solution-focused strategies to resolve staff conflicts.

In Chapter Eleven, teachers will find solution-focused strategies for handling difficult parent-teacher interviews, and for working with problem students. Chapter Twelve shows how to set up solution-focused anger management groups, parenting groups, counselling groups for children, and programs for aggressive youth. Worksheets are provided (in the appendices) to guide you in using solution-focused counselling techniques.

Start at the beginning, or pre-read a chapter that piques your interest. Either way, I hope the material will engage you and inspire you to use the solution-focused model.

ONE

The Solution-Focused Model

Suppose, that one night, while you were asleep, there was a miracle and this problem was solved. How would you know? What would be different?

(de Shazer, 1988)

The solution-focused model began in the late seventies as a form of brief therapy. Use of this form of therapy blossomed as practitioners saw tangible, quick results. Today, the solution-focused model has changed the way many therapists think about problems, and how to help their clients. It has been used extensively with a wide range of problems, including: addictions (Berg & Miller, 1992), eating disorders (McFarland, 1995), mental health problems (Rowan & O'Hanlon, 1999), sexual abuse (Dolan, 1991), children's problems (Selekman, 1997), and adolescents' problems (Selekman, 1993).

More recently, solution-focused ideas have been applied to school problems (Durrant, 1995; Metcalf, 1995). As the model became well known, teachers and principals realized that the concepts and strategies would be helpful to them in their work with students and parents.

The solution-focused model is different from traditional problem-focused models. It is a *solution-building* model, which requires a shift in the way we think.

This chapter compares the assumptions underlying traditional problem-focused models and the solution-focused model. Problem-focused questions are compared with solution-focused questions, which have a different focus and effect. A case example shows how solution-focused questions can quickly shift a meeting from problems to solutions. Finally, a chart of assumptions is included to help you understand the differences between the two paradigms.

Differences Between Models

PROBLEM-FOCUSED MODELS emphasize the importance of obtaining an extensive history of the problem. Time is spent chronicling when and where the problem has appeared. Problem-focused questions are used, and the emphasis is on the search for *causes* of the problem or the "why" of the problem. Problem-focused models are deficit and pathology-oriented. They have the following underlying assumptions (adapted from O'Hanlon & Wiener-Davis, 1989):

1. Insight is necessary for change to occur
2. Change will take a long time
3. We need to know the cause of a problem in order to fix it
4. We need to know the entire history of a problem in order to solve it
5. Complex problems need complex solutions
6. The role of the professional is to identify and correct deficits.

Assumptions, like those above, are pervasive in North American culture. They are so common we no longer think of them as assumptions. For example, in counselling sessions, students or parents automatically begin to tell the entire history of the problem and what they believe are its causes. They may spend an entire meeting talking about what is wrong.

The more they reiterate the history of the problem, the more they become problem-saturated. This constrains them from seeing their strengths and resources. They look to the professionals as experts who will provide them with solutions.

Furthermore, school meetings tend to focus on the history of the student's problem, the student's deficits and possible causes of the problem behaviour. The assumption is that once problems and deficits are identified, a plan can be then generated to correct the student's deficits and weaknesses.

The solution-focused model operates from a different set of assumptions about problems and change (adapted from O'Hanlon & Wiener-Davis, 1989). It assumes:

1. Students and parents have resources
2. Change is constant and inevitable
3. We don't necessarily need to know the entire history of the problem in order to solve it
4. It is not always necessary to know the cause of a problem in order to solve it
5. One small change leads to bigger changes
6. Rapid change is possible
7. Students and parents are capable of generating solutions that fit their needs
8. The role of the professional is to identify and amplify change.

As you can see, the solution-focused model operates from a different paradigm. The way you think about problems and change will determine the types of questions and strategies that you use.

Problem-Focused Questions versus Solution-Focused Questions

IN THE DEVELOPMENT OF THE solution-focused model, Steve de Shazer, Insoo Kim Berg and their colleagues (1985) examined the interview process. They noticed that most of the questions used in interviews were problem-focused. They began to think about how therapists could use questions differently – to focus on strengths and to construct solutions. A turning point came when de Shazer (1985) asked a client, "What is happening when the problem isn't there?" This question changed the focus for both the interviewer and the client.

The team developed a simple schema for understanding the difference between problem-focused and solution-focused questions. Reportive questions are used to get a history of the problem and the person's perception of the problem. Constructive questions are used to construct goals, solutions, and to highlight strengths and resources. Table 1.1 (de Shazer & Lipchik, 1986) summarizes the distinction between the two types of questions.

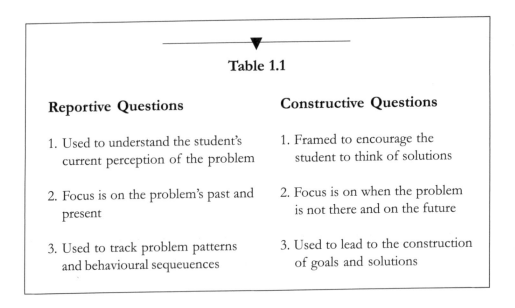

Table 1.1

Reportive Questions	Constructive Questions
1. Used to understand the student's current perception of the problem	1. Framed to encourage the student to think of solutions
2. Focus is on the problem's past and present	2. Focus is on when the problem is not there and on the future
3. Used to track problem patterns and behavioural sequeuences	3. Used to lead to the construction of goals and solutions

Reportive Questions

Most professionals have been trained to ask reportive questions. We have been trained to ask about the history of the problem, problem patterns that have occurred over time and the student's understanding of the problem. The focus is on the problem in the past and present:

> *What sense do you make of that?*
>
> *What's it like for you when you feel you can't do well in school?*
>
> *When did you notice that your problems began?*
>
> *How long has the problem been going on?*

Some have been trained to track relationship problems in the student's social system. These questions are used to assess how families and school professionals are caught in a pattern that sustains the problem:

> *When your son doesn't do his homework, what do you do? What does his father do?*
>
> *Of all of the family members, who is having the hardest time with dealing with your son's learning difficulties?*
>
> *When the student lost his temper, what did you do? Then what happened?*

Constructive Questions

Constructive questions are used to construct goals and solutions, and to elicit strengths and resources. These were later referred to as solution-focused or solution-oriented questions. There are two major types of solution-focused questions: *exception-finding* questions and *future-oriented* questions.

Exception-finding questions are used to explore times, in the past and present, when the problem is less frequent, or when it is not there. Student strengths and resources, no matter how small, are highlighted:

When have you done better in school?

What helped you to get your homework done last week?

How did you manage to show up for school two days this week?

Exception-oriented questions focus on what was different in the student's social system when things were better:

When things were better, what were you doing? What was your teacher (friends, parents) doing?

If your friends were here, what would they say helped you to keep on going?

Suppose your teacher were here. What would she say helps make things better in class?

Figure 1.1 describes the process of identifying and amplifying exceptions. By asking exception-finding questions "holes" are being poked into the problem picture. Possibilities and resources begin to emerge.

The Milwaukee team discovered that future-oriented questions are another way to elicit solutions. They were working with a difficult client who insisted that the only thing that would help her would be a miracle. The interviewer asked her, "Suppose this miracle happened, what would be different in your life?" She stopped venting and began to describe how she wanted her life to be (Berg, 1998, p. 77).

▼

Figure 1.1
Exception and Future-Oriented Questions

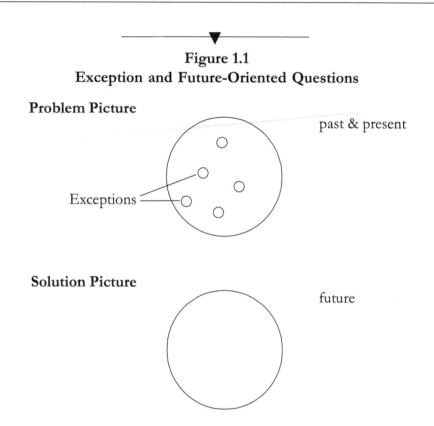

Problem Picture

past & present

Exceptions

Solution Picture

future

The team was so impressed with the details of her miracle picture they began to use this question with other clients. The *miracle question* is now a hallmark of the solution-focused model (de Shazer, 1988).

Future-oriented questions are used to help the student visualize what life will look like when the problem is solved or when the situation is improved (Figure 1.1). Most students and parents have never thought about this future picture because they have been focused on the problem picture. Future-oriented questions include the following:

> *How will you know when he is doing better?*

> *What will be signs to you that he is improving?*

> *Suppose school is going better for you,
> what will that look like?*
>
> *Suppose the problems you are worried
> about are solved, what will be happening
> when things are better?*

Future-oriented questions can be used to track solution patterns in the student's social system:

> *Suppose things are better between you
> and the teacher, what will that look like?
> What will the teacher be doing? What will
> you be doing?*
>
> *When the problems are solved, what will
> you be doing? What will your parents
> (friends) be doing?*
>
> *Suppose your friends were here, what
> would they notice is different about you
> when the problem is solved?*

Both reportive and solution-focused questions are useful. However, if we use only reportive questions, the problem picture continues to remain the focus. How can we shift a meeting from problem talk to solution talk? The following case example highlights how solution-focused questions changed the course of an interview.

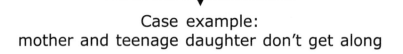

Case example:
mother and teenage daughter don't get along

Karen requested a meeting because of ongoing conflict with

her teen-age daughter, Sarah. During the meeting, they angrily blamed each other for their difficulties. They wanted to give me the entire history of their problems, and what they believed was wrong with the other person.

After listening to their frustrations, I asked:

> *Suppose, that tonight while you are sleeping, a miracle happens, and the problems that brought you here are solved. The miracle happens while you are asleep, so you don't know it has happened. When you wake up tomorrow morning, how would you know that the miracle had happened? What would be different?*

The mother and daughter stopped venting and were silent. They slowly began to describe what it would look like after the miracle. Their tone of voice softened, and they began to talk about times when they used to get along. They both became committed to making their miracle picture happen.

At the end of the meeting, I gave them a solution-focused homework task. I asked them to take two days in the next two weeks and pretend that the miracle had happened. On these days, they were to act as they would on the miracle day, and notice what was different on the miracle days. They also had to guess which day the other had picked as her "miracle day" and to write down what was different about the other.

Two weeks later, Karen called me and said, "That was a sneaky thing you did!" She continued, "We've been pretending the miracle days and now we don't need to pretend. The miracle days are happening. We don't need to come back for a second session." I asked her:

> *On a scale of 1 to 10, and 10 means that*
> *things are the way you want them to be,*
> *where would you put today?*

She replied "an 8." I then asked her:

> *On the same scale, and 10 means that*
> *you are confident that you can keep these*
> *changes going, where are you today?*

She confidently stated, "an 8." I complimented her on their progress and agreed that they didn't need another meeting. I assured her that they could return should they require further assistance. This is a typical solution-focused interview. As you can see, changes happened quickly.

The Solution-Building Process

THERE ARE THREE KEY QUESTIONS that the solution-focused model uses in the solution-building process:

1. Exception-finding questions
2. Future-oriented questions
3. Scaling questions.

Each of these questions is covered in more detail in subsequent chapters. This section describes the solution-building process, using the idea of feedback loops. Feedback loops are used to diagram patterns in relationships (Tomm, 1985). Figure 1.2 shows the basic elements of a feedback loop.

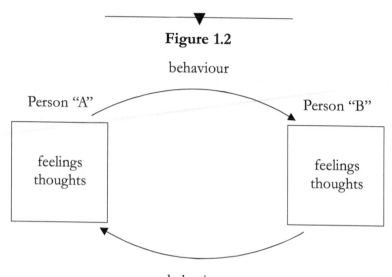

Figure 1.2

behaviour

Person "A"   Person "B"

feelings
thoughts

feelings
thoughts

behaviour

In the previous case example, if I had tracked the problem pattern occurring between the mother and daughter, it would have looked like this.

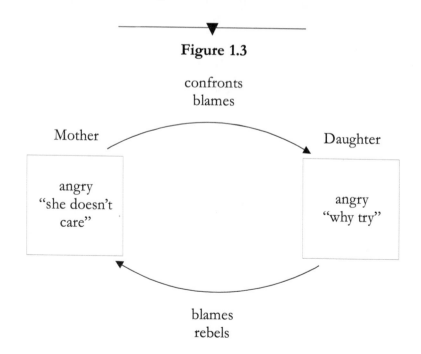

Figure 1.3

confronts
blames

Mother   Daughter

angry
"she doesn't
care"

angry
"why try"

blames
rebels

If this problem pattern occurs frequently, it will become a dominant pattern in the mother/daughter relationship. If one thinks linearly and looks at only one half of the feedback loop, it would be easy to blame either the mother or the daughter for their relationship problems. However, human relationships are not linear. Circular thinking explores how both the mother and the daughter help maintain the problem. Both parties are caught in an escalating problem pattern.

There are six possible points of entry for changing the feedback loop. The mother can change her feelings or thoughts towards her daughter. Or, she may decide to react differently to her daughter. Similarly, the daughter can make changes in her thoughts or feelings about her mother, or change her reaction to her mother. It does not matter where they begin. One small change in the feedback loop will lead to other changes, leading to a ripple effect of changes.

The solution-focused model emphasizes building solution patterns. During my meeting, I didn't spend much time asking the mother and daughter about the problem pattern. I simply asked them to imagine the miracle picture and helped them to describe the solution pattern (Figure 1.4).

Figure 1.4

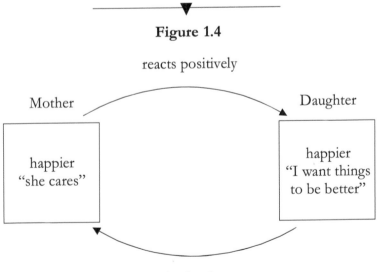

reacts positively

Mother

Daughter

happier
"she cares"

happier
"I want things
to be better"

tries harder

Train yourself to think in terms of these feedback loops. They will help you to amplify exceptions and expand the solution picture. If the significant people in the student's life are not physically present, you can bring them into the room with questions. For example, if I had met only with the daughter, I would have asked the following questions:

> *Suppose your mother was here, what would she say it would look like after the miracle?*
>
> *What would she say would be different about you after the miracle?*
>
> *What would you notice would be different about her?*
>
> *Suppose your friends were here, what would they say would be different between you and your mother?*

Notice that these questions expand the solution picture by asking about change as seen through the eyes of her mother and her friends. These relationship questions are an essential skill in the solution-building process. As you read the case transcripts throughout the book, notice how the solution pattern is systematically constructed through the use of relationship questions.

▼

Table 1.2
(adapted from Durrant, 1995; Metcalf, 1995)

Traditional Assumptions About School Problems	Solution-Focused Assumptions About School Problems
The cause of the problem must be found in order to solve it.	A problem can have many causes. It is more helpful to look at how we can get change started.
The student needs to work through underlying issues before she/he can change.	Change starts now, with small changes leading to big changes.
Insight is necessary for change to occur.	Insight is not necessary for change to occur, and it often occurs after a change in behaviour.
Students are resistant to change.	Resistance is not a helpful concept. If we expect resistance, we will see more of it.
Counselling needs to be long-term and change will take a long time.	Rapid change is possible.
We need to identify and correct student deficits.	Students have resources and it is more helpful to focus on what they are doing right.
Students must want to change before they can be helped.	Students are more motivated when they are involved in defining goals that fit for them.

TWO

How to Become Solution-Focused

We achieve what we expect to achieve and what others expect us to achieve.

(Adapted from Rosenthal, 1968)

A teacher's belief in a student's ability can be a significant determinant of outcome. When teachers believed that their students would do well on an IQ test, those students scored 25 points higher on their tests than other students with different teachers (Bennis, 1976 cited in Selekman, 1993, p. 31).

Similarly, studies of counselling outcomes show that the counsellor's belief in the client's ability to change can be a significant determinant of treatment outcome (Selekman, 1993, p.30). It is clear that our beliefs about students and parents affect our work with them. But, how can one develop a positive expectancy of change and convey this to students and parents?

This chapter focuses on key assumptions underlying the solution-focused model. Practicing the solution-focused model does not simply mean using some solution-focused questions. Adapting to this new model involves a paradigm shift away from the "typical" way of thinking.

Ten Solution-Focused Guidelines

The following section features ten guidelines that will help you to become a solution-thinker (adapted from O'Hanlon & Weiner-Davis, 1998). We will look at how these guidelines can be implemented to your work with students and parents:

1. When students ask for help, they are already changing
2. Change is constant – there are always exceptions
3. Students are already doing something right to solve their problem
4. A single session can promote change
5. A positive expectancy leads to change
6. You don't need to know the entire history of a problem in order to solve it
7. You don't need to know all the causes of a problem in order to solve it
8. Behaviour is best understood in its context
9. Students are more likely to change when they feel validated
10. Students are more motivated when they generate solutions that fit for them.

1. When Students Ask for Help, They Are Already Changing

You may have had the following experience. A student, who is in crisis, asks to meet with you. However, you are unable to see him immediately, so you schedule an appointment for later in the week. As the time of the meeting draws near, the student reports that he doesn't need to see you because things are better. While waiting to meet with you, he has solved the problem. This phenomenon is called pre-treatment change – when a person asks for help, the process of change has already begun.

The Brief Family Therapy Center conducted a research study on pre-treatment change with clients who had asked for counselling (Weiner-Davis, de Shazer, & Gingerich, 1987). In the first meeting, interviewers began the meeting with a pre-treatment change question:

> *We've noticed that after people make a phone call for an appointment and by the time they come in for the appointment, many people report that things are already a little bit better or different in their lives. What kinds of things have you noticed that are a little bit better since you called?*

Notice that this question orients clients towards exceptions. Clients expectι to be asked about the history of the problem, not when things were better!

The clients began to think about small changes since their request for the appointment. For example, clients with addiction problems reported that they had cut down on their use of drugs or alcohol since asking for the appointment. Depressed clients noticed that they felt a little bit better. The interviewer then amplified these exceptions with questions, such as:

> *How did you manage to get that to happen?*

What made things a little bit better?

What else helped?

After exceptions were identified and explored, the interviewer asked a solution-focused scaling question:

On a scale of 1 to 10, with 10 standing for the problems that brought you here are solved, and 1 standing for how bad things were before you made the phone call, where would you put yourself today?

Sixty percent of the clients reported that they were at 3 on the scale, and ninety percent reported that they were above 1 on the scale. In the next stage of the interview, pre-treatment changes were further amplified:

How did you get to 3 or 4 on that scale?

What did your family do?

What else helped?

Any positive or useful action by the client was highlighted. The final questions focused on how to help the clients build on the changes they had made:

How will you know that you have moved up one notch on the scale?

What will be happening in your life?

At the end of the meeting, clients were given compliments and a solution-focused homework task:

We are very impressed regarding the changes you've noticed and what has helped you move up to a 3 on the scale.

> *You've done a lot of work already. In the next two weeks keep track of what's helping you stay at 3 and what helps you move to a 4. Write that down, don't talk about it, and bring the list back to the next meeting.*

After this process of solution-focused questioning, some clients reported that they were doing better than they realized and they decided that they didn't need a second meeting.

Implications of Pre-Treatment Change For School Counsellors

A junior high school counsellor asked me for advice on how to handle her high caseload demands. She felt guilty when she was unable to see students on the same day they requested her help. I reminded her of the concept of pre-treatment change and how she could build on it.

I recommended that she use a quick assessment process to assess the severity of a student's problem. If it was a serious problem, then of course, the student should be seen immediately. For students with less serious problems, I recommended that she give them the following solution-focused task before their first meeting with her:

> *I would like to meet with you on (appointment day). Until we meet, I'd like you to think about when things have been better for you and write these things down. For example, if it is a problem with your teachers, write down when things have been a little bit better for you in school. What has been different about the teachers or about you? Bring your list to our first meeting. This will help me to help you.*

The counsellor was astonished by how many students reported pre-treatment change. Now, she consistently elicits pre-treatment changes, explores what helped, and what needs to happen for the changes to continue. Before ending the meeting, she uses scaling questions to determine the student's sense of progress and confidence in keeping change going:

> *On a scale of 1 to 10, and 10 means the*
> *problem that brought you here is solved,*
> *and 1 means the opposite, where would*
> *you put yourself today?*
>
> *On the same scale, 10 means that you*
> *are confident that you can keep these*
> *changes going, and 1 means the opposite,*
> *where are you today?*

Students who report a high number on the scales of progress and confidence often need only one session. The counsellor likes the solution-focused model because she feels less pressure to be the expert who has to come up with the solutions. Students leave her sessions feeling empowered in their ability to solve their problems.

2. Change is Constant – There are Always Exceptions

When one is in the middle of a problem, it's easy to develop a "problem-saturated" view of a situation (White, 1986). The student who is a troublemaker always seems to be the troublemaker. The difficult parent always seems to be difficult. This problem-saturated view creates difficulties when the professional is unable to see exceptions to the problem. Train yourself to listen for and search for exceptions. Exceptions are times in the past and present when things were better in the student's life. Finding exceptions helps to poke holes in that problem picture. These openings are the beginning of solutions and possibilities.

Case example:
he's always bad

A family was referred for counselling because their teen-age son was skipping school. In the first interview, the parents began to list a series of complaints about their son. After listening to their concerns, the conversation flowed as follows.

———•———

Counsellor: It sounds like you've been through a lot. **(validating)** Can you tell me, when were things a little bit better?

Mother: Not much! He only went to school one day last week.

Counsellor: He went to school one day last week? Really! How did he get himself to school that day? **(identifying exceptions)**

Mother: Ha! He probably went because his friends were going to school that day.

Counsellor: But still, he could have skipped all five days. I'm really curious about this.

Counsellor: *(to son)* How did you decide to go to school that day? How did you get yourself out of bed and get there? It would have been easier to skip all five days. **(amplifying the exception)**

Son: Well, we had a really important test that day and I knew that if I didn't write it, things would be really bad.

Counsellor: So you don't want to have things get worse?

Son: Are you kidding?

Counsellor: Well, some young people don't care.

Son: No way, I'm in enough trouble as it is.

———•———

In this dialogue, I elicited and amplified exceptions and did not, as he expected me to, focus on his problem behaviour. This also helped to shift his mother's focus – currently on his irresponsible behavior – on to his responsible behaviour. This is the beginning of the solution-building process.

3. Students Are Already Doing Something Right to Solve Their Problem

Students are already doing *something* right to solve their problem. However, students, parents and teachers often don't recognize this because they are focused on the problem picture. We need to ask questions that will help promote the idea of strengths and solutions. The following scenario demonstrates how I used solution-focused questions to focus on what the sixteen-year-old was doing right.

Case example: how did you manage to throw down the knife?

Counsellor: How did you decide to set up this meeting today? **(focusing on strengths)**

Mother: Well, my kids were fighting. *(The son and daughter are present for the interview. There is a feeling of tension and the son doesn't want to look at me).*

Counsellor: What happened?

Mother: Well, they had an argument.

Counsellor: Yes, then what?

Mother: They were fighting, as they usually do, and then my son got mad. He picked up a knife and went after my daughter with it.

Counsellor: Then what happened?

Mother: Well, he chased her and then he threw down the knife and went outside and trashed the shed. Totally smashed it.

Counsellor: *(turning to son)* How did you manage to do that?

Son: *(sullenly)* What? *(Now he is more involved in the interview)*

Counsellor: How did you manage to throw down the knife? **(focusing on an exception)**

Son: *(surprised)* I don't know.

Counsellor: But how did you manage to throw down the knife? Some people, when they are in that state of anger, don't throw down the knife. That's how people get hurt or killed. How did you manage to throw down the knife? **(amplifying the exception)**

While listening to the mother's problem description, I was impressed with the fact that the young man did something right: he threw down the knife. This question took him by surprise. He thought I was going to focus on the history of all his problems. He became more involved in the interview process and was later willing to discuss what changes he needed to make.

Focusing on exceptions helped the family to recognize that he stopped his violence before it became worse. They felt more hopeful that he could change. The rest of the meeting focused on their goals and what safety plans needed to be put in place for all family members.

4. A Single Session Can Promote Change

As I became more proficient in the solution-focused model, I noticed that some clients didn't return for their second appointment. I thought I had done something wrong. When I made a follow-up phone call, they reported that things were better and that they didn't need to come back! I didn't know how to make sense of this until I read the book *Single Session Therapy* (Talmon, 1990).

A common assumption is that counselling needs to take a long time. However, research shows that clients can benefit from a single session (McConkey, 1997; Talmon, 1990). Talmon studied an agency's appointment statistics, which summarized the number of sessions counsellors had with their clients.

He reviewed 100,000 scheduled appointments over a five-year period. He was surprised to find the most frequent or modal number of sessions that staff held with clients was one session. Many clients simply didn't return for the second scheduled appointment. Others were offered a second appointment, but the clients chose not to meet again. Furthermore, they chose a single session even though there was no fee for the sessions, and they were not interested in seeking counselling elsewhere.

After reviewing the statistics, he talked with the staff about these single-session clients. The staff described these clients as dropouts, not motivated, resistant to change, or not receptive. The staff also wondered whether they themselves had done something wrong in the interview, such as failing to establish rapport with the client.

Talmon then did a client satisfaction survey with 200 of these single-session clients. Seventy-eight percent reported satisfaction with a single session. They reported changes in the problem that led them to seek counselling and in other areas of their life. Only ten percent of the clients reported that they didn't like the counsellor or the outcome of the single session. The remaining clients gave practical reasons for why they hadn't returned for the second appointment.

Talmon reviewed the literature and found other studies that confirmed his research. One study looked at client dropouts after one session at a community health center. It concluded, "Almost 80 percent of the clients interviewed reported that their problem(s) had been solved" (cited in Talmon, 1990, p.10).

Slive and his colleagues (1996) describe how they offer single-session counselling in a walk-in clinic, located in a shopping mall. The clinic is operated on a walk-in, first-come, first-served basis. Clients are offered the opportunity to have further sessions, or they may choose to have a single session. An independent evaluation showed that 89% of the clients were satisfied with the service after one session.

Implications of single session counselling for school professionals

Talmon's research shows that you are likely going to have only one session with a student or parent. How can you make the most of that session? It would not be helpful to spend most of the meeting taking a history of the problem. Being effective in a short amount of time is critical.

Solution-focused language and questions generate strengths, resources and solutions quickly. When you build on pre-treatment change, a single session can rapidly move the student to solutions. Furthermore, single-session counselling frees up resources for students who need more time and assistance.

Single-session counselling focuses on achievable, realistic steps to help the student get back on track. The student may return for another single-session later. Sometime, your single session may be an assessment and referral. For example, the student may need an assessment for learning disabilities. If there are issues of abuse or violence, the appropriate authorities must be notified. A follow-up call or talk is still important to assess how the student is progressing.

5. A Positive Expectancy Leads to Change

The following story demonstrates how our beliefs about students influence our perception and our behaviour. At the beginning of the school year, a principal called three teachers into her office for a meeting and explained:

> *As a result of your teaching excellence over the last three or four years, we have come to the conclusion that you are the best teachers in this school. And as a special reward to you, we have identified three classes, each with thirty of the brightest students in this school – the students with the highest IQs. And we're going to assign them to you to teach for the entire year.*
>
> *Now, we don't want to be accused of discrimination, so it's very important that you do not tell these children in any way that you know that they've been selected for a screened class. And second of all, we're not going to tell their parents, because we don't want to cause any difficulties there.*
>
> *I expect you to teach exactly the same way you normally do and use exactly the same curriculum, and I expect you to get very good results with these students.*

The results were that these students led not only the school, but also the entire school district in academic accomplishment. Their grade levels were twenty to thirty percent above the grade levels of the entire school. At the end of the year, the principal had another meeting with the teachers:

> *Well, you've had a very good year.*
>
> *Yes, we have... it was so easy, replied the teachers. These children were so bright. They were so eager to learn, it was such a pleasure to teach them.*
>
> *Well, maybe I'd better tell you the truth, said the school principal. This has been an experiment, and those ninety children were chosen out of the school population at random. When I assigned them to your class at the beginning of the year, I had no idea what their IQs were.*
>
> *That's incredible, exclaimed the teachers. But how could it be that they scored so highly? They did so well! They*

got such good grades! It must be because we are such excellent teachers.

To which the principal said, I think I should also tell you the other side of the experiment. At the beginning of the school year, we put all the teachers' names in a hat, and yours were the first three names drawn.

Dr. Howard Rosenthal of Harvard University performed this experiment in a San Francisco Bay area school. He repeated this experiment 300 times, each time getting similar results (Rosenthal & Jacobson, 1968).

These average students did so well because of the positive expectancy of the teachers. The principal expected the best from the teachers who did their best as well. We achieve what we expect to achieve and what others expect us to achieve.

6. You Don't Need to Know the Entire History of a Problem In Order to Solve It

Have you ever been to a meeting to discuss a problem student? These meetings often dwell on the student's deficits, the history, and possible causes of the student's problems. By the time participants get around to brain-storming solutions, the momentum is often lost and people leave these meetings feeling hopeless.

You don't need to know the entire history of a problem in order to solve it. The solution-building process can begin with exception-finding questions:

> *When was the student doing better?*
>
> *What has worked so far?*
>
> *When are the problems less frequent?*

Many of the case examples in this book show how to create change simply by asking future-oriented questions. These questions help the person to shift from the problem picture to the solution picture:

> *Suppose school is going as best as possible, what will that look like?*
>
> *What will be signs to us that you are serious about making things better?*
>
> *What do the other students need to see to convince them that they can trust you?*

7. You Don't Need to Know All of the Causes of a Problem in Order to Solve It

A problem can have many causes. When one becomes solely focused on searching for all of the causes, one can feel increasingly immobilized. Simply asking future-oriented questions can create change.

This is not to say that causes should be ignored. For example, a student may have medical or biological problems that need to be assessed and treated. When there are medical or biological problems, parents, teachers and students may feel they have no influence over the problem. How can professionals help them to regain some sense of control in their lives?

The next case example illustrates how a client felt increasingly immobilized by focusing on the causes of her medical problem. She found ways of improving her health, when she began to focus on the exceptions.

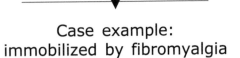

Case example: immobilized by fibromyalgia

A woman in one of my workshops asked me how the solution-focused model could help with medical problems. She told me she had been diagnosed with fibromyalgia. Medical professionals had given her many different opinions about the causes of her illness. She felt increasingly confused and immobilized about what to do.

I suggested that she keep track of when her symptoms were less intense or frequent and write down what was different at those times. She was amazed at what she discovered. She noticed that when she was having fun or doing things she enjoyed, the symptoms were hardly noticeable. When she was feeling stressed, the symptoms escalated.

As a result of her findings, she began taking steps to care for herself by doing things she enjoyed and increasing her support system. Later, she changed her job for a less stressful one.

8. Problem Behaviour Makes Sense When It Is Understood in its Context

Problem behaviour makes more sense when understood in its context. For example, if a student doesn't do her homework, you may become frustrated and begin to think of her as lazy or not interested.

However, if you knew she has lost a family member recently, you would see the behaviour differently. You would see her behaviour as a natural reaction to grief and would be more patient with her. Always try to back up and look at the problem in the context of the "bigger picture."

9. Students are More Likely to Change When They Feel Understood and Validated

Students are more likely to consider change when they feel validated and understood. Resistance and defensiveness are reduced when we show that we are genuinely interested in how students perceive their situation. The following case example highlights how important it is to validate the current reality the student faces.

Case example:
what's good about drugs?

I was asked to meet with a teenager because he was using drugs and this was affecting his schoolwork. It was tempting to assume an authoritative stance and lecture him on the dangers of doing drugs. But I knew this would alienate him. I had to do something different to capture his attention, so he would be receptive to ideas I would propose later.
In a genuine, interested tone of voice, I asked:

How is using drugs helpful?

He was surprised by this question. I said that most people do something for a reason, so there must be a good reason why he is doing drugs. He talked about how drugs helped him to feel confident, more outgoing, accepted by his peers, and helped him forget his problems.

I then asked in the same interested, non-judgmental tone of voice:

How is using drugs not helpful to you?

He said that he had got in trouble with the law; that drugs created problems for him at home and at school; and he was worried that he may become addicted.

If I had confronted the student about his drug use or lectured him about its hazards, he would have become defensive and resistant. After I listened to his opinions about drugs, he felt understood and not judged. He was then more open to exploring their negative consequences. He was not prepared to give them up totally, but he was willing to modify his use of them. He decided that he would not use drugs before or during school. For him, this was a big change.

10. Students are More Motivated When They Generate Solutions that Fit for Them

Too often, the goals educators set with students reflect what *we* think they should accomplish. The more students are involved in the goal-setting process, the more likely they are to follow through with the action plan. In the previous case example, the student generated solutions that worked for him. I could not force him to stop using drugs. He was more likely to modify his use of drugs if he generated the solutions. Remember, one small step will lead to bigger changes.

THREE

How to Shift from Problems to Solutions

Aim your eyes to where you want to go.

Many years ago, I took lessons on how to drive safely in icy, winter conditions. The instructor emphasized, "If you look at the tree you think you are going to hit, you will hit it. Aim your eyes to where you want to go." When we are problem-focused, our attention is on the tree we think we are going to hit. When we are solution-focused, we aim our eyes to where we want to go.

The first part of this chapter describes guiding principles (de Shazer, 1989) that will help you to stay solution-focused. The second part describes how you can use future-oriented questions to help students and parents aim towards the solution picture.

Four Guiding Principles

1. Find Out What the Student or Parent Wants

Usually, students and parents are focused on what they *don't want* in their life: "He won't bug me all the time," "We won't fight," "You won't pick on my kid." They're not as clear about what they *do want*. They have difficulty answering future-oriented questions because they have not thought about the solution picture. They have been more focused on when the problem occurs. This chapter describes how to use future-oriented questions to help students and parents construct solutions:

> *What will it look like when things are better?*
>
> *Suppose the problem is solved, what will be different in your life?*

2. Find Out What Is Working

Exception-finding questions are used to elicit strengths, resources, coping strategies and previous solutions. When you use these questions with parents and students, focus on times when there has been some progress. Chapter Four describes how to focus on these small islands of competence and build on them.

> *I noticed you handed in your assignments last month. What helped you then?*

3. Do More of What is Working

When you find out what works, then do more of it. Assigning solution-focused tasks (Chapter Eight) helps to build on what is working and helps the student sustain changes.

This week, keep track of what helps you to complete and hand in your assignments.

4. If What You are Doing is Not Working, Do Something Different

This guideline seems to be common sense, but we often do the contrary. For example, parents persist in lecturing their teen, even when it isn't working. Teachers continue to confront students on their problem behaviours. Over time, the attempted solutions become part of the problem.

If what you are doing is not working, do something different. Use different teaching strategies, or approach the student in a different way. Solution-focused questions and tasks can be helpful in doing something different. Start by reviewing the first guideline – find out what the parent and student wants.

The Miracle Question

Suppose, after we talk today, when you go home and go to bed tonight, during the night, a miracle happens. All of the problems that brought you here are solved. Now, since you are asleep, you don't know this miracle has happened. When you wake up in the morning, how will you know the miracle has happened? What will be the first sign? (de Shazer, 1988)

The miracle question is a powerful question that helps you, students and parents to shift from being problem focused to solution focused. Students and parents become very intrigued with this question, even if they don't believe in miracles.

Notice how the question is worded. Initially, the student is not asked to do anything differently. As the student listens to the question, he begins to mentally shift with the direction of the question: after we talk today *(yes)*, when you go home *(yes)*, and you go to bed tonight *(yes)*. We gently lead the student from the problem picture to the solution picture.

It is important to take your time when asking this question because the student needs time to shift his thinking. When using the question, pause between each phrase:

> *Suppose... after we talk today... when you go home ...and go to bed...and during the night... a miracle happens...all of the problems that brought you here are solved... When you wake up in the morning how will you know that the miracle has happened? ...What will be the first sign? ...*
> ***(silence)***

There are many ways to introduce this question:

> *I'm going to ask you an unusual question, one that will help me to understand how I can help you.*

> *I'm going to ask a strange question, one that will take some imagination on your part.*

Allow silence and time for the student to absorb the question. Often, students will initially respond with "I don't know." This is a reasonable response, because they haven't thought about it. Gently persist with the question in a number of ways:

I'm just asking you to suppose for a moment. I'm not sure it's going to happen yet, just suppose for a moment. What will be the first thing you would notice that is different in your life?

What would your mother (father, friends, children, etc) notice after the miracle? What would I notice?

Many interviewers have difficulties expanding the miracle picture. The student may describe an unrealistic picture or is unable to describe what he would be doing differently. Persist in tracking the solution pattern feedback loop. Here are some suggestions:

What would be the first sign that the miracle had occurred? What else?

Suppose these changes happened, what would be different in your life?

What would others notice?

Young children may not understand the word "miracle." You can adjust the wording of the question to their developmental level:

Suppose after we talked today, I waved a magic wand, and all of the problems that brought you here, are solved. What would be different in your life? How could you tell that the problems are solved?

Suppose the good fairy came and sprinkled fairy dust all over your house (classroom, school, family) and solved all of the problems, what would be different?

A school principal uses these questions when young students are sent to his office for misbehaving in the classroom:

> *Suppose I were a fly on the wall in your classroom. What would I see that would tell me things are going better for you in class? What would you be doing when things are better?*
>
> *What would your teacher be doing when things are better?*

Children have a great imagination and respond to these questions because the questions are non-threatening. Frequently, I have obtained more information about problems in a child's life with future-oriented questions, than with problem-oriented questions. For example, one young boy responded, "My daddy wouldn't be drinking." Until then, I was unaware he had concerns regarding his father.

If the word *miracle* doesn't fit, you can use other future-oriented questions. You can simply ask the student to *suppose* his problems are solved.

> *Suppose the problem is solved. What would be different? How would you know it was solved?*
>
> *What would be the first sign?*
>
> *Suppose your teacher did change, what would be different about her? And when this change happens, what would your teacher say would be different about you?*

The word *suppose* is a beautiful word. It is a non-threatening way to help the student imagine the solution picture. When the student begins to describe the imaginary picture, he is already changing his thoughts about the situation. You can overcome a student's hesitation to answer the question by saying:

Just suppose for a moment. I'm not sure all of this will happen, but just suppose things are better. What will be signs that it is getting better?

A crucial component in asking future-oriented questions is to have the student or parent describe the solution picture with concrete, observable signs of progress. You should have a good idea of what the solution picture will look like in their daily life. If you don't, then you need to ask more questions. For clarity, systematically track the solution pattern feedback loop, as described in Chapter One.

Students and parents will frequently base their ideas for change on the absence of the problem picture. They may say, " He won't be acting up" or "My parents won't be nagging me." It is difficult to build solutions on what *won't be* happening. Train yourself to ask: What *will be* happening instead? The following case example shows how to systematically build a solution pattern and to elicit observable signs of progress.

▼

Case example:
mother and daughter don't get along

This is a continuation of the case example described in Chapter One. Notice how I am persistent in asking them for small, concrete and observable signs of their miracle picture.

Counsellor: So, what will it look like after this miracle?

Daughter: She wouldn't be nagging me all of the time.

Counsellor: What would she be **doing instead?**

Daughter: She would be nicer.

Counsellor: How could you tell when she is nicer?

Daughter: She would say hello and smile at me when I come home from school. Right now, she just grills me about school.

Counsellor: What else will it look like **when** things are better?

Daughter: We would do some of the fun things we used to do.

Counsellor: What kinds of things?

Daughter: Shopping, going to a movie. She's always so stressed out and doesn't have time.

Counsellor: Suppose you start doing these things, how will that help?

Daughter: We would get along more.

The remainder of the interview focused on their miracle picture and signs of progress. The solution pattern they described is shown in Figure 3.1.

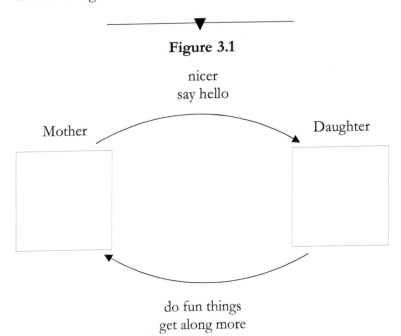

Figure 3.1

nicer
say hello

Mother   Daughter

do fun things
get along more

Goal-Setting

WHEN YOU ARE ADMITTING A STUDENT to a program or special class this is a wonderful opportunity to involve the student and parents in goal setting. Some introductory questions might be:

> *How will you know that this program has been helpful? What will be different about you (your marks, your life) at the end of this program?*
>
> *How will you know you are ready to leave this program?*
>
> *When you are ready to move on from here, what do you think people will notice about you that is different?*
>
> *If we make a videotape of you now, and then another videotape of you when you are ready to leave here, what will be different on the second video? How could we tell which is the second video?*
>
> *How will you know when your daughter is ready to leave this program?*

Goal Setting in Parent-Teacher Interviews

Some teachers struggle with how to deal with meetings that involve angry, venting parents. It is often difficult to direct volatile meetings towards a more constructive direction. These meetings can result in an escalation of blame, anger and defensiveness by all parties involved. Here are some ideas for shifting the meeting from problem talk to solution talk:

> *We both want things to be better for your child. In order to make the most of this*

*meeting, I'm going to ask you an unusual
question. How will you know, by the time
that you leave here today, that this
meeting has been helpful? What will be
signs that we are on track?*

*When things are better, what will your
daughter be doing? What will I be doing?
What will the school be doing? What will
you be doing?*

*We have half an hour today to discuss
how to help your son. If we need more
time, we can schedule a later meeting.
How will you know this meeting has been
helpful?*

*What will be signs, after you leave today,
that things are a little better?*

Using Scaling Questions to Set Goals

Parents, students and teachers like scaling questions because they are visual
and concrete. They are wonderful tools for setting meeting goals and for
designing a student's Individual Program Plan (IPP). Let's say you have a
concern about a student's reading progress. You can set goals with the student
using scaling questions:

*On a scale of 1 to 10, where 10 means
you are reading as best as possible, and 1
means the opposite, where would you put
yourself today? What helped you to get to
that number? When have you been higher
on the scale? What was happening then?*

*On a scale of 1 to 10, where 10 means
that you are making friends, and 1 means
the opposite, where are you today? What
is helping? What will help to move it up*

*one notch? What will you be doing? What
will the other children (your parents,
teacher) be doing?*

When you use scaling questions, it is important to keep the discussion positive and non-evaluative. Even if the student responds with a 2 on the scale, do not give up. Ask the student: What has helped you to get to a 2? When have you been higher on the scale? More ideas on how to use scaling questions are described in Chapter Five.

How to Negotiate Achievable Goals with Students

When setting goals, it is important to elicit achievable, observable signs of progress. Ask yourself: Am I clear what it will look like when the problem is solved? How will I know that I have helped the student? Can I help the student meet the goals she has set or are they too big?

If you are not clear what the solution picture will look like in the student's daily life, ask more questions to obtain concrete, observable and behavioural indicators of change. Use the following seven guidelines to keep on track when negotiating goals with students, parents, or teachers (adapted from Berg & Miller, 1992).

Ensure the goal is important to the student

It seems self-evident that the goal needs to be important to the student. However, school meetings often focus on what *we* think should happen. For example, if a student's goal is "to get the teacher off my back," that may be the goal you start with. Resist your desire to confront the student. When the line of questioning focuses on the student's goal, the student is more likely to be cooperative:

*Suppose the teacher is off your back?
What difference will that make for you?*

What else will it look like when things are better in school?

When the teacher is off your back, what will be different about you when things are better?

Aim for small rather than large goals

For example, it is unrealistic to expect a student to change all of her problem behaviour. It is more realistic to focus on times when the student is doing better in school. It may be too much to ask a frustrated teacher to be more positive with a difficult student. However, the teacher may be willing to keep track of when things are a bit better with this student.

If a student has a substance abuse problem, it may be unrealistic to ask him to give it up. It may be more realistic for him to keep track of when he is overcoming the urge to use. Aim for small rather than large goals. Achieving small goals will create a ripple effect of other changes.

Obtain specific, concrete and observable indicators of progress

When you are asking a student or parent to describe the solution picture, obtain specific, concrete, observable signs of progress:

What will be the first sign to the teacher that you are serious about making things better?

What will be signs to you that the student is doing better?

How we will we know we are making progress with this student? What will we see him doing in the classroom?

Focus on what will be happening

This guideline is one of the most crucial things to remember when helping students and parents describe their solution picture. Their initial reaction to solution-focused questions tends to come from the problem picture: "I won't do drugs," "We won't fight any more," "The teacher won't yell at me." They describe change based on the absence of the problem.

It is very difficult to build a solution picture based on what "won't be" happening. Train yourself to ask about the presence of solution behaviour. For example, a teacher may say that when things are better, the student would stop being disruptive. Ask what *will be* happening instead?

Parents complain that their children are always fighting and their miracle is "that the kids won't be fighting." You need to ask for concrete, observable signs of progress:

> *What will be happening instead of fighting?*
> *What will the children be doing instead?*
>
> *What will be signs to you that the children are getting along? What will they be doing?*
>
> *When they are getting along, what will be different about you? What will they notice about you when things are better?*

Build solution patterns

Focus on building the beginning of solution patterns rather than ending problem patterns. It is easier to ask a student to start something new or different, rather than trying to stop the problem behaviour. For example, think about a habit that you are trying to change, such as smoking or over-eating. The more you focus on not having cigarettes or eating your favourite foods, the more deprived you feel and the stronger the craving becomes. Rather than focusing on stopping a problem habit, focus on a positive goal, such as feeling healthier and more energized. Once attention is directed towards these new goals, positive habits can be built.

Elicit realistic and achievable steps towards change

When obtaining details of the miracle picture, help the student describe the solution picture with realistic and achievable signs of change:

> *What will be the first sign that you are doing better in the classroom? What will the teacher notice you are doing?*

> *What will help you keep your temper in its place? What will you be doing?*

> *What will your teachers (parents, friends) be doing that will help?*

Frame the goals as involving effort or hard work

The solution-focused approach can bring about change very quickly and the student or parent may attribute all of these positive changes to you. Consequently, they may doubt that the changes will last, or may not be confident in their ability to maintain the changes. During the meeting, or when suggesting a homework task, emphasize it will take some effort by them to make the changes happen:

> *You are right, this will take some effort on your part.*

> *This goal is worth working hard for, because you want things to be better.*

> *It will take some willpower, on your part, to overcome the urge to use marijuana at school. You said it would be worth it because you want your parents off your case and to trust you more.*

When you first begin to use future-oriented questions, they may seem a bit strange or unwieldy. There is no need to memorize the questions. The simplest way to learn this model is to build on the skills you already have. You already know how to get a history of the problem. Use the same skills and get a *history of the future.*

How to Develop a Cooperative Relationship with Parents and Students

WHEN WORKING WITH DIFFICULT STUDENTS or parents, it is easy to take a linear view and label them as resistant. However, we can try to break this pattern by asking, how can I adjust myself to the stance of the student so that I am more effective? There are three types of working relationships educators may have with students. The salient difference between the three types is the participant's readiness for change (de Shazer, 1985; Berg & Miller, 1992).

Customer Relationship

In a customer relationship, the person wants change and is willing to do something about the problem. For example, a student who asks you for academic help is a customer for doing better in school. Parents who ask for advice are customers. They want to know how they can help their child more effectively. The parent is ready for suggestions and willing to follow through on them. In a customer relationship, the person wants change and is ready to change her part of the feedback loop. At the end of the meeting, she/he is ready for an action-oriented task.

> *You have really good ideas about what helps to make school go well. Do more of these things and keep track of what else helps.*
>
> *I am glad that you asked for some ideas. Here is what I would suggest...*

Complainant Relationship

In a complainant relationship, the person wants change but is not prepared to do something about it. Complainants focus on how someone else should change first. Complainants are not ready to look at how they may be part of the problem pattern or part of the solution.

It is not useful to give an action-oriented task to complainants at the end of a meeting, because they are not ready. Instead, give them an observation task. These are outlined more fully in Chapter Eight:

> *In order to help me with my assessment, keep track of times when this student is doing better in your class. Notice what he is doing or what you are doing.*

> *In the next week, keep track of when things are better at home. Notice what your parents are doing. Parents, keep track of what your daughter is doing. Write these things down and bring your lists to the next meeting.*

Visitor Relationship

In a visitor relationship, the person who you are meeting with has not requested the meeting. Frequently, someone else sends students to the counsellor or the principal. The student says, "I don't have a problem. The teacher thinks I have a problem. I don't know why I'm here." In a visitor relationship, the student initially does not identify a goal or a problem with which he needs help. Ideas for how to work with visitors are more fully elaborated in Chapter Nine.

When working with a student, with whom you have a visitor relationship, listen for the *hidden customer*. For example, a teen may not be a customer for doing better academically, but he may be a hidden customer for "getting my parents off my case." He may be willing to work on a goal that is relevant to him. A student with an eating disorder may not be a customer for changing her eating patterns, but she may be a customer for staying out of the hospital. A more cooperative relationship is developed when we work on a goal relevant to the student.

> *It sounds like things have been tough for you. It's clear that you would like to have the teacher and your parents off your case.*
>
> *You don't think that you have an eating problem, but it's clear that you don't want to be admitted to hospital. What would it take to show them that you can keep yourself healthy?*

Future-oriented questions help to draw out the hidden customer. Many times, a student has entered my office as a visitor and left the meeting as a customer for changing something that is important to him. Solution-focused questions help to create motivation, reduce defensiveness and to create hopefulness.

FOUR

Exception-Finding Questions:
How to Build On What Works

Find out what is working. Do more of it.
(de Shazer, 1985)

I worked with a young student who had temper problems. She hit and kicked children, swore in class, and required many time-outs. After I talked with her for a while, I asked her when things were better in school. She replied that she only had one time-out in the previous week, but "nobody noticed." I asked her how she managed to have only one time-out. The remainder of the meeting focused on other times when she was managing her temper.

Find out what is working and have the student do more of it. My young client's parents and teacher hadn't noticed when she was managing her temper. They were more focused on when she was losing her temper.

Search for Islands of Competence

IN THE SOLUTION-FOCUSED MODEL, OUR TASK is to watch and listen for exceptions, strengths and resources. In some cases, the signs will be very small. Every exception is a potential key to a solution:

> *How did you manage to come to school today?*
>
> *Two weeks ago, you handed in your homework. What helped you then to finish your work?*

The first skill is learning to recognize exceptions. Unless you make this part of your thinking, you won't recognize the small steps a student is taking. Watch and listen for exceptions, no matter how small.

Some teachers and counsellors are able to identify exceptions but do not know how to expand on them. This chapter describes different ways to ask about exceptions and how to build on them.

There are two types of exceptions, *deliberate* or *random* (de Shazer, 1988, p.4). Some students can identify what has helped them when things were better in school or when their life was better. These are *deliberate* exceptions.

Of course, students and parents do not come to a meeting with a list of these exceptions. Solution-focused questioning directs their attention to when things were better and what helped. In these situations, you just need to find out what was working and then have the student do more of it.

Other students may not be able to identify what helped to make things better in the past. One student told me that sometimes he "just has a good luck day." He could not identify anything that helped these days to go better; he believed the exceptions were a fluke. These exceptions are termed *random* or *spontaneous.*

It is important to explore both kinds of exceptions as they can both lead to possible solutions. After I explored what was different about the student on his "good luck day," it became clear that he was doing many things to improve his situation.

Six Ways to Ask About Exceptions

USE THE FOLLOWING SUGGESTIONS TO UNCOVER and amplify exceptions (Berg & Miller, 1992):

1. Use indirect compliments
2. Search for exceptions
3. Explore previous solutions
4. Amplify pre-treatment change
5. Explore the ending of problem sequences
6. Ask coping and surviving questions.

1. Use Indirect Compliments

It isn't enough to simply get a list of exceptions. A key component in solution building is to amplify these with the use of indirect compliments. Most people are more familiar with direct compliments, when the student is praised for his effort. Some students do not respond to praise because of self-esteem issues or because they don't trust the sender's motives.

Indirect compliments can be more effective because the student has to stop and think about what he was doing that was useful. When the student talks out loud about what is working, this further consolidates his success.

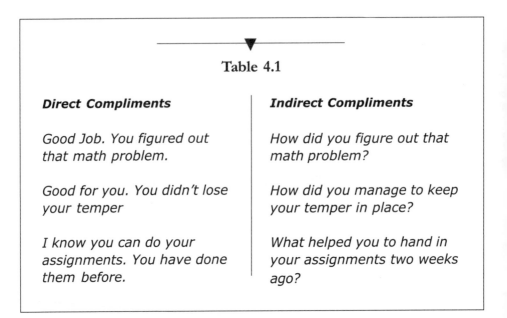

Table 4.1

Direct Compliments	*Indirect Compliments*
Good Job. You figured out that math problem.	How did you figure out that math problem?
Good for you. You didn't lose your temper	How did you manage to keep your temper in place?
I know you can do your assignments. You have done them before.	What helped you to hand in your assignments two weeks ago?

2. Search for Exceptions

The following questions help to elicit exceptions, and are useful in case conferences, parent-teacher meetings, and consultations:

When is the problem less severe? When is it less frequent?

When are the times when the problem isn't there?

What is different about the times when things are better?

How did you (they, the student, parents) get that to happen?

Who noticed that this time was different?

3. Explore Previous Solutions

One girl told me that when she gets upset, she talks to her cat. This provided me with an opening to discuss how this helps her, and what else has helped her. Sometimes, all that is necessary is to ask the student to recall previous solutions to other problems:

> *Have you ever had this problem in the past? How did you solve it then?*
>
> *What will you need to do to have that happen again?*
>
> *How have you solved other problems?*

When people are in the middle of a problem, they are not focused on existing competencies or how other problems were solved. When providing consultation to teachers or parents, these questions can be very useful to elicit solutions:

> *You've dealt with other tough kids before. What worked then?*
>
> *What has worked with your son in the past?*

4. Amplify Pre-Interview Change

When students and parents ask for help, they are already changing. They have decided to talk with someone about their problem. These requests for help are opportunities to build on change that is already occurring:

> *How did you decide to ask for help?*
>
> *How did you decide that this was the time to do something?*

Often, people notice that things are better between the time they call for the appointment and the time they come in for the meeting. What have you noticed that is better since you made the phone call?

Suppose these changes continue, what difference do you think this will make in your life?

▼

Case example:
I want you to see my daughter
for counselling right away!

A school counsellor shared this dramatic example of pre-counselling change. A parent called to complain about her adolescent daughter's behaviour and wanted the counsellor to see her daughter immediately.

The counsellor said she would try to see the daughter that week. However, because of her heavy schedule, she wasn't able to meet with the daughter. The mother, unaware of this, assumed that the daughter had seen the counsellor.

The following week, the mother reported to the teachers that she was noticing many changes in her daughter! This is a great example of pre-interview change. The mother began to look at her daughter differently because she assumed that change was taking place.

5. Explore the Ending of Problem Sequences

Most of us remember how problems start but do not pay attention to how they end. Think back to an argument you have had with a loved one. We are more likely to dwell on what began the argument rather than how it ended. Exceptions can be found in the ending of problem sequences:

> *How did you manage to stop fighting? What did you do? What did other people do?*
>
> *How did the tantrums stop? What did your child do? What did you do?*
>
> *How did you decide to come back after running away? Some kids wouldn't bother.*
>
> *How did you end the binging and purging when you did?*
>
> *How did you stop using cocaine after three days? You could have continued.*

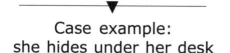

Case example: she hides under her desk

A teacher asked me for ideas regarding the behaviour of a grade two student. Whenever the student became upset, she hid under her desk. Later, on her own initiative, she came out from under the desk and rejoined the class.

As the teacher described the situation, I listened for exceptions. I was impressed that the little girl was doing something good for herself. When feeling threatened, she took care of herself by hiding under her desk. Furthermore, I was impressed that the girl later joined the class when she felt ready. She was able to end the problem sequence. This was another sign of her strengths.

I suggested that the teacher have a conversation with the girl and ask the following questions, with a genuine, curious tone of voice:

> *How do you know when it's time to go under your desk?*
>
> *What kinds of signals do you have in your body or in your head that tell you it's time to hide?*
>
> *What is happening in the class that tells you it's time to hide under your desk?*
>
> *What helps you while you are under your desk? What do you think about or do?*
>
> *How do you know it's time to come out from under your desk? What signals do you have in your body or in your head that tell you it's okay to join the class?*
>
> *What is happening in the class that tells you it's safe?*

These questions highlight the student's resources. Notice that this line of questioning also helps the teacher shift from a negative to a positive view of the student's behaviour. The teacher's initial view was that the girl's behaviour is a problem. By exploring with the student how the behaviour helps, the teacher can begin to view the behaviour as a resource.

Most likely, hiding under the desk helps the student manage anxiety or fear. She is a hidden customer for feeling safe. The teacher can now help her to look at other ways she manages anxiety:

> *You aren't hiding under your desk all of the time. What helps you in class when*

you aren't under your desk? What are you doing then?

What else helps to make the class go better for you? What are the other kids doing?

6. Ask Coping and Surviving Questions

These questions are helpful with students who are dealing with family problems such as alcoholic parents, a chronically ill family member, or little family support for the student's academic efforts. In these situations, teachers may feel angry towards the parents and powerless in being able to help the student. Coping and surviving questions can be used to enhance the resiliency of these students:

How do you manage to cope with such a difficult situation?

A lot of people in your situation would have given up. How do you keep on going?

Knowing what it has been like for you, how do you motivate yourself to get to school every day?

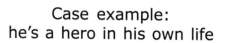

Case example: he's a hero in his own life

A grade nine drafting teacher asked me how to deal with a student in his class who was not paying attention, was not completing his homework, and was in danger of failing the subject.

I asked him to tell me more about the student as a person. In the last parent-teacher interview, he found out that the student's girlfriend just had a baby. The student wasn't sure if they were going to keep the baby, nor was he clear about his role in the child's life.

I told the teacher I was impressed that this student continues to attend school in spite of the major events that have happened in his life. He has become a father, and he isn't sure of his parenting role at this point. In spite of all this, the student continues to attend school. Drafting class probably isn't a priority in his life at this moment and yet he continues to show up.

After listening to my comments, the teacher paused and said, "You know, the more you talk, the more I am beginning to think that this student is a hero, not a failure!" My comments helped him reframe his view of this student. Now he can approach the student from a resource view as opposed to a deficit view. This new frame will be reflected in his tone of voice and how he deals with the student.

I recommended that the teacher meet with the student at the end of class and have the following conversation to highlight the student's coping skills:

> *I've been thinking about the meeting I had with your mother and I wanted to say that there seems to be a lot happening in your life right now. **(validation)***
>
> *Knowing what you are going through, how do you get yourself to school every day?*
>
> *How do you manage to concentrate in school or in my class? What helps? What are you doing, what am I doing, what are your parents (friends, girlfriend) doing that helps?*

After initiating a more positive teacher/student interaction, the teacher can then shift to future questions:

> *Suppose drafting class was going as best as possible, what would that look like? What will I be doing? What will you be doing? What else will be happening when the class is going better?*
>
> *What will it take to get through the class so that you don't fail the subject? What can I do to help? What can you do?*

Enhance Students' Resiliency

WHAT HELPS STUDENTS SURVIVE AND DEAL with difficult circumstances? For decades, social research focused on factors that damage people, such as poverty, racism, abuse, neglect and illness. In counselling, clinical research focused on pathology, not health, and many conclusions were drawn from small samples taken from clinical caseloads.

Research did not study those who do not come to professional attention and who solve difficulties on their own. Pathology-oriented research failed to explain how some people remained well adjusted or how some people turn their lives around.

One famous longitudinal study began to change this focus. Emily Werner and Ruth Smith (cited in Ah Shene, 1999) studied the entire population of children who were born on the island of Kauai in 1955. The researchers tracked the children from birth to their early thirties. One-third of the population of children were identified as "high-risk."

These children had many risk factors in their lives such as poverty, discord, substance abuse or mental illness in the family. By the time they were ten years old, two-thirds of these high-risk children had serious learning or behaviour problems. By age 18, many had mental health problems, juvenile delinquency records, or pre-marital pregnancy. However, by their early thirties, most of the high-risk children who had developed problems had turned their lives around (Ah Shene, 1999).

The remaining third of the high-risk children grew into competent, caring adults and did not have the serious childhood and adolescent problems of their counterparts. The researchers were interested in what factors had helped these children overcome difficult circumstances. They looked at factors internal to the child, and external factors in the environment.

Internal Factors

Werner and Smith noted that even in infancy there was something different about the high-risk children who did not develop serious problems. They were active, affectionate, good-natured infants and alert and autonomous toddlers. Resilient children tend to have the following traits (cited in Ah Shene, 1999).

Social Competence

> They attract positive attention, are empathic, communicate well and can find humour in difficult situations.

Problem-Solving Skills

> They can plan, think critically and creatively, and seek help when needed.

Critical Consciousness

> This allows them to be aware of the problems in their family or society and to know they are *not* the cause of these troubles.

Autonomy

A belief that they can influence events around them, a strong sense of their own identity, a sense of purpose and a belief in a bright future.

Recruitment of Support

Resilient children often recruited support from friends, teachers and other elders. They joined organizations such as the YMCA, and took advantage of educational opportunities at colleges, in religious or community service organizations.

The researchers concluded that resilient children were not unusually gifted. They were effective in using the abilities they had and in taking advantage of the supports their environment did offer.

External Factors

When the resilient adults were asked what helped them to overcome their difficult circumstances, the majority stated that they had one adult in their childhood who cared about them as a person. This adult may have been a teacher, a loving parent, or someone in the community.

Prevention programs can have an enormous impact on enhancing students' resiliency. A study of the Big Brothers/Sisters mentoring program showed that the "Littles" were 46 percent less likely to start using drugs, as compared to a control group (Ah Shene, 1999). The results were even better for minority children.

Prevention programs can help children be more successful. The Perry Preschool Project in Michigan worked with children who were at risk for school failure (Ah Shene, 1999). The preschool gave the children the chance to plan, solve problems, make decisions, and initiate their own learning, in an environment that allowed high interaction with adults.

Follow-up research showed that these children were significantly less likely to become pregnant, commit crimes, and were more likely to graduate from high school, start post-secondary education or find a job. At age 27, this group showed less criminal activity (7% versus 35% in the control group). The study demonstrated that chances for success are enhanced with as little as one or two years of exposure to a planned prevention program.

Helping students enhance their resiliency can be one of the most important things you do. The solution-focused model offers you the practical tools to do this. Exception-finding questions draw forth strengths, resources and successes. The miracle picture and other future-oriented questions draw forth possibilities. We can enhance resiliency by seeing students in terms of their strengths, and by approaching them with a belief in their abilities.

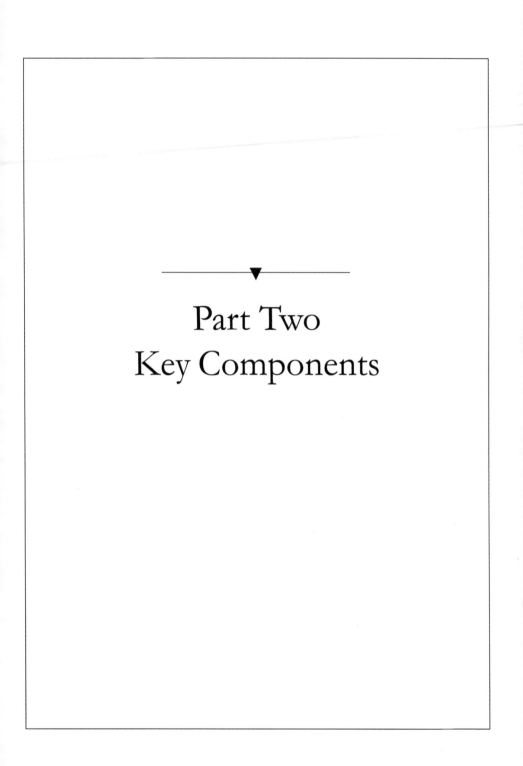

Part Two
Key Components

FIVE

Scaling Questions: How to Build Solutions Step by Step

On a scale of 1 to 10, and 10 means the problem is solved and 1 means the opposite, where would you put yourself today? What has helped you to get to that number? What will help it to move up one notch?

(Berg, 1994)

S caling questions are the easiest way to begin to use the solution-focused model. They are simple, versatile, and effective. This chapter covers different types of scaling questions and how they can be used in the classroom, in meetings with students, and in parent-teacher interviews.

Scaling questions are not to be used as an evaluative tool that compares the student to a norm. They are tools to clarify goals, and to draw forth strengths and resources. Overall, the process for using solution-focused scaling questions is pretty simple. Table 5.1 sets out the basic process.

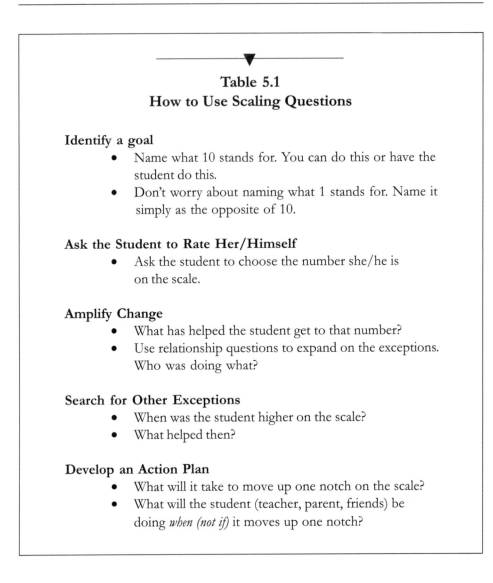

Table 5.1
How to Use Scaling Questions

Identify a goal
- Name what 10 stands for. You can do this or have the student do this.
- Don't worry about naming what 1 stands for. Name it simply as the opposite of 10.

Ask the Student to Rate Her/Himself
- Ask the student to choose the number she/he is on the scale.

Amplify Change
- What has helped the student get to that number?
- Use relationship questions to expand on the exceptions. Who was doing what?

Search for Other Exceptions
- When was the student higher on the scale?
- What helped then?

Develop an Action Plan
- What will it take to move up one notch on the scale?
- What will the student (teacher, parent, friends) be doing *when (not if)* it moves up one notch?

Seven Useful Scaling Questions

AN ENTIRE MEETING CAN BE CONDUCTED USING scaling questions, or one can use them in a quick ten-minute problem-solving talk with a student. This section outlines the most commonly used scaling questions and how they can be used in different situations (Berg & Miller, 1992). Scaling questions can be used to:

1. Assess a student's motivation
2. Assess a student's confidence in change
3. Assess a student's progress
4. Work with different beliefs about a problem
5. Establish goals with students, teachers and parents
6. Conduct a quick interview
7. Assess levels of safety and suicidal risk.

Let's look at different scenarios to see how versatile and useful scaling questions are. In the case examples, notice how the use of scaling questions helps to build motivation and hope.

1. Assessing the Student's Motivation

On a scale of 1 to 10, with 10 meaning you'll do anything to solve these problems, and 1 meaning that you're not sure, where would you put yourself today?

It is more useful to use this scaling question at the end of a meeting, rather than at the beginning of a meeting. During the meeting, solution-focused questions help build motivation and a sense of hope. At the end of the meeting, a student is more likely to respond with a higher number on the motivation scale.

Your tone of voice is important. If you ask the question in a frustrated, challenging tone of voice, the student will become defensive. Pose the question in a genuinely curious, non-judgmental tone of voice, regardless of what number the student gives.

This scaling question also helps you assess the type of relationship you have with a student. Do you have a visitor, complainant or customer relationship?

The type of homework task you suggest will depend on the student's readiness for change.

For example, if the student states that she is at an 8 out 10 in motivation, most likely you have a customer relationship, and the student is likely ready for suggestions or an action task. If the student says she is at a 2, most likely you have a visitor relationship and the student will not be ready to consider the changes she needs to make.

In these situations, you need to move more cautiously – resist the temptation to push the student for change. Instead, search for a goal that is meaningful to the student.

2. Assessing the Student's Confidence in Change

*On the same scale, and 10 means you are
confident that you can solve this problem,
and 1 means you're feeling pretty shaky,
where would you put yourself today?*

Some students are very motivated to solve their problems. However, they may not feel very confident that they can solve their problems. Motivation and confidence are not the same thing. For example, a student with alcoholic parents may rate herself as very high in wanting the problems solved. However, she may rate herself as 2 out of 10 in her confidence that the problems will be solved.

The following case example shows how scaling questions, regarding motivation and confidence, motivated a young adult to change her behaviour. This case example also shows what to do when there are different levels of motivation among family members. Some members may be highly motivated and confident that changes can be made, while other family members may rank themselves lower on the scale.

▼

Case example:
I don't think it will change

This was an initial meeting with two parents and their adolescent daughter. I thought the session had gone well. All of them seemed to be thoughtful and motivated after the miracle question. At the end of the session, I asked them scaling questions regarding motivation and confidence:

Counsellor: Now, I am going to ask you another unusual question. On a scale of 1 to 10, where 10 means you will do anything to make things better at home, and 1 means that you aren't sure, where would you put yourself today?

Mother: I'm at an 8

Father: Me too. It can't continue the way it has.

Counsellor: *(to the daughter)* And where would you put yourself on the scale?

Daughter: Well, to be honest, I'm at a 4. *(After hearing this, the parents are in despair.)*

Counsellor: I appreciate you are being honest about this. What do you see that makes you more cautious than your parents?

Daughter: Because I don't think this counselling will work.

Counsellor: Oh. So you aren't hopeful or confident that counselling will help.

Daughter: Right.

Counsellor: Right now, I'm not asking about confidence that the counselling will work. I'm just asking about how much you want things to be better at home.

Daughter: Oh, I'm at a 6 in wanting things to be better. I'm just not sure we can do it.

Counsellor: So you are a 6 in wanting things to be better, and a 4 in confidence that things can get better.

Daughter: Yeah.

Initially, the daughter responded with a lower number because of her feelings of hopelessness that things would change. Once I rephrased the questions, she was clearer that she wanted things to change at home, but she wasn't confident that they would. The next step was to build her confidence in the counselling process and that change could happen with her parents.

Counsellor: What will it look like when it moves up one notch in your confidence that this counselling will work?

Daughter: Well right now, when I get home from school, the first thing my mother does is grill me about my day at school, did I do my work, who did I talk to, and on and on.

Counsellor: So, what will be different when it moves up one notch? What will happen instead?

Daughter: I would come home, go to my room to unwind, and after half an hour, I would come upstairs to talk.

Counsellor: That's all?

Daughter: Yes that would be a start.

At the end of the session, I complimented the parents for their willingness to listen to their daughter, and the daughter for being honest about her worries about the counselling process. I commented that they were all unhappy with their family life and wanted to be happier.

For the next week, I asked them to keep track of what helps to move them up one notch on the scale. The daughter was to write down what she noticed her parents doing to help move it up one notch. Similarly, the parents were to do the same regarding their daughter and each other. I asked them not to discuss their lists with each other, and to bring their lists to the next meeting.

Notice that I adjusted the homework task to their readiness for change. The daughter was a complainant, focusing on how her parents should change. She wasn't ready to look at how she could change her behaviour. It was difficult for her to refuse the task because she only needed to observe what her parents were doing to make things better. At the same time, she knows her parents will also be observing her. Consequently, she most likely will make some changes in her behaviour. She will want to make sure that they will have something to write on their lists!

3. Assessing the Student's Progress

> *Suppose you were at a 1, when we started the tutoring, and 10 stands for you don't need to see me any longer, where would you say you are today?*

When I am not clear about a parent's or student's goals, I use this scaling question to get their sense of progress. The question can be framed in many different ways:

> *On a scale of 1 to 10, 10 means that the problem that brought you here is solved, and 1 means how things were before we started to meet, where would you put yourself on the scale today?*

> *On a scale of 1 to 10, and 10 means that you are reading as best as you can, and 1 means the opposite, where would you put it today?*

> *On a scale of 1 to 10, and 10 means that you are ready to come back into class, and 1 means the opposite, where would you put yourself?*

To prepare a student for the end of counselling, I ask:

> *Suppose you were at a 1 when you first began to meet with me, and 10 means that you no longer need to come and see me, where would you put yourself today?*

> *What would be a good enough number on the scale for this problem to be solved as best as possible?*

Most students are realistic and say, "If I can get to a 6 or 7 and not let it go below 4 very often, I'll be doing great!"

▼

Case example:
we haven't dealt with grandma's death

This case example shows how a scaling question was helpful

in unlocking hidden issues in a family. I had been working with 17-year old Sandra, who was referred to me by her parents.

They were very angry with her and, initially, not willing to attend the meetings. They complained that Sandra stayed out until two in the morning, hung around with undesirable friends, and her marks were rapidly dropping. They had made it clear to her that they were "at the end of their rope" and they might have to ask her to leave home if she didn't improve.

Sandra compliantly attended the first two meetings, but I could tell she was not invested in the process. In the third session, I asked a scaling question to clarify her goals for counselling.

———————

Counsellor: You have been very responsible in attending; this tells me that you don't want to further jeopardize things at home. And it seems to me that you want to stay at home, at least long enough to complete high school. Yet, I don't think these meetings are getting at what you need. I have a very clear idea of what your parents want but I'm not sure what you want. Let me ask you, on a scale of 1 to 10, 10 stands for the problems in your family are solved, and 1 stands for the opposite, where would you put things today?

Sandra: It's at a 4.

Counsellor: What has helped get it to a 4?

Sandra: Since I've been coming here, my parents are off my back a little bit.

Counsellor: What will it look like, in your eyes, when it has moved up to a 5 or 6?

Sandra: We will talk about my Grandma's death.

Counsellor: What do you mean?

———— • ————

At this point, Sandra told me about a very stressful period in her family's life. When she was thirteen, her father was hospitalized for a very serious illness. At the same time, her maternal grandmother, with whom she was very close, unexpectedly died. The funeral was held in another city and she and her sister were not allowed to attend.

In her mind, the family had not been the same since. Her father had a long recovery and her mother, burdened with the stress of her husband's illness and her mother's death, distanced herself from her daughters.

As she told me this, Sandra became very sad and wept. I suggested that she had been carrying her and her family's pain alone for too long. I asked her to invite her family to the next session.

The family discussion was very moving and meaningful, as they talked about that difficult time in their lives. I commended them on the hard work they had done. I asked Sandra,

> *What will help to move up one more notch in making things better in the family?*

She replied that she wanted go to her grandmother's grave and to have the funeral ritual that they had yet to have as a family.

This was the last session I had with Sandra and her family. In a follow-up call, the mother indicated that Sandra was doing better in school, seemed much happier, and was coming home on time. They were planning when they would visit the grandmother's grave.

4. Working with Different Beliefs About A Problem

If your teacher (parents, friends, probation officer) were here, where would they put you on the scale?

Students, teachers and parents may have different opinions about a problem. Instead of trying to get everyone to come to an agreement about the problem, you can work with the differences with a scaling question. The next case example shows how a teacher used the progress scaling question to work with parents who disagreed with her concerns about their son's reading abilities.

Case example: a reading problem

Linda, a grade five teacher, had been working very hard to motivate Jeff to improve his reading skills. She was frustrated and believed that neither he nor his parents seemed to be as concerned about his reading as she was. She requested a meeting with Jeff and his parents to discuss her concerns. She decided to use a scaling question to clarify their goals for Jeff's reading skills.

Teacher: Thank you for coming to this meeting. As I mentioned to you on the telephone, I'd like to discuss how to help Jeff improve his reading skills. In order make the best use of our time, I'd like to ask all of you a question that will help me to understand how you see the situation.

Parent: All right.

Teacher: On a scale of 1 to 10, 10 means that Jeff is reading as best as possible, and 1 means the opposite, where you would you put it today?

Parent: We'd put it at a 6.

———•———

The teacher is surprised at this number because she believes that Jeff is at a 2 out of 10. She decided to explore their reasons for ranking it as 6 out of 10.

———•———

Teacher: Wow! That's a high rating! What has helped to get it to a 6?

Parent: Well, last year he wouldn't even pick up a comic. Now, he reads them a lot.

Teacher: Now that you mention it, I've noticed that Jeff brings his comics to school. *(Until now, she had felt negatively about the comics.)* Jeff, what are your favourite comics?

Jeff: Superman and Batman.

Teacher: What do you like about them?

Jeff: They're really strong and they get to do really exciting things. Not like school, school is boring.

Teacher: Sometimes school seems boring to you. Suppose we could make it a little more exciting and interesting, what would that look like? **(goal setting)**

Jeff: I would be able to do things that I like to do.

Teacher: Like what?

Jeff: At home, I like to build models and other things with Dad.

Parent: It's true; he is really good with his hands. If you give him a choice between reading and building things, he'll choose building activities any day.

Teacher: *(to Jeff)* So, you are a doer! Later, we can figure out how we can bring in your building interests to help school be more interesting.

Teacher: Jeff, on that same scale, 10 means you are reading as best as possible, and 1 means you are not, where would you put yourself today?

Jeff: I'd say an 8!

———•———

Again, the teacher thinks this number is inflated. However, she continues to explore his rating to better understand his perception.

———•———

Teacher: What has helped to make it an 8?

Jeff: Reading comics and other things that I like to read. Last year, the teacher wouldn't let me read them at school.

Teacher: Of course. It makes sense that you do better when you read things that you are interested in. What else do you like to read?

Jeff: Action war stories. The school stories are so boring.

Teacher: What have your parents been doing to help it get to 8?

Jeff: They ask me about the book I am reading. I get to tell them what I like.

Teacher: Jeff, when is it lower on the scale?

Jeff: I don't like it when we have to read out loud in front of the class. Everybody laughs. It's so stupid.

Teacher: So you don't feel so good when you have to read out loud. That's understandable. When else is it lower on the scale?

Jeff: I don't understand the words. Some of them are too big.

Teacher: What is the number on the scale when you are having trouble?

Jeff: It's a 2.

The scaling questions helped the teacher to change her view of Jeff and his parents. Initially, she viewed reading comics as uncooperative behaviour, but, during the conversation, she realized that they help him to build his confidence in reading. She also realized that, when he was asked to read in front of the class, his defiant behaviour was really a sign of anxiety. The teacher, parents and Jeff talked about what would help to move him up one step on the scale and generated an action plan.

5. Establishing Goals

Suppose 10 stands for the problems are solved, and 1 means the opposite, where are you today on this scale? What will it look like when you move up one notch?

This scaling question is useful for quickly establishing goals with teachers, parents and students. The following excerpt is a conversation between and a principal and a student at the beginning of the school year.

▼

Case example:
I'm on probation

Students with behavioural problems often have a history of failure. It is crucial to involve these students in goal setting and to explore what has or hasn't helped them. Notice that the principal focuses on goals that are meaningful to the student, rather than immediately focusing on the school's expectations of the student.

Principal: I wanted to meet with you today to get your ideas about how we can help make this year as best as possible for you. I would like your opinion on what has been most helpful to you and what hasn't been helpful to you. That way, we can build on what helped and not make the mistakes that you think were made in the past. How will you know this school year will be going as best as possible for you? **(goal setting)**

Student: *(sullenly)* I wouldn't be here.

Principal: Sure. **(validating)** It sounds like school is not your favourite place to be. Let me ask a question that will help me to understand how we can best help you make it through this year. On a scale of 1 to 10, 10 stands for school is going as best as possible, and 1 stands for the opposite, where would you put it today?

Student: It's a 2.

Principal: What has helped get it to a 2? **(amplifying exceptions)**

Student: What do you mean? Two means that school stinks.

Principal: Sure. What have you been doing to keep it from getting worse?

Student: I have to be here as part of my probation.

Principal: So, you are making sure that you don't break probation. **(exception finding)** How come?

Student: I don't want to go back to the place where they sent me before. **(hidden customer)**

Principal: That makes sense. So, knowing you don't want to be here and knowing that you feel school stinks, how will you know it has moved up one notch on the scale? **(goal setting)**

Student: Teachers won't be on my case. At the last school, they hounded me to get my work done. I know when things are due.

Principal: So, hounding you doesn't work. What will they be doing instead?

Student: Just telling me the date and I'll figure out how to hand it in.

Principal: That would help it to move up one notch?

Student: Yeah.

Principal: It also sounds like you are trying to stay low because of the probation order. (building on the student's goal) How will the probation officer know it has moved up one notch? **(amplifying change)**

Student: That I show up here every day. I have to go to court at the end of the month.

Principal: So they will want some kind of record stating that you have been attending regularly.

Student: Yes.

Principal: What will it take in the next two weeks to help you to attend regularly? What will you be doing and what will we be doing?

Student: I'll show up, and the teachers won't need to be on my back.

———•——

Initially, the student was a visitor for attending school. As the conversation proceeded, it became clear that he was a hidden customer for meeting the requirements of the probation order. The principal aligned himself with this stance and adjusted his questions to the student's goal.

It was premature to expect the student to become a customer for doing better academically. The initial step was to make school bearable for the student and to draw on his ideas. Hopefully, he will begin to shift his stance as he feels more positive in the school.

At the end of the meeting, the principal took a think break (see Chapter Six), to show the student that he was genuinely interested in what the student had to say. The think break was a surprise to the student and a meaningful intervention in itself. The student had never had anyone take a break to consider what he had said! The principal shared the following message:

> *I am impressed with how honest you have been and that you showed up for this meeting even though it wasn't your idea.* ***(compliments)***
>
> *I'm sure that you have had more than your share of meetings over the years. It is very clear to me that you want to meet the*

requirements of your probation order and that attending regularly will help. You also stated that it would help if the teachers do not hound you. **(bridging statements)**

During this week, keep track of everything that is helping to move things up one notch on the scale. Keep track of what the teachers are doing, what other students are doing, and what you are doing. Write these things down, don't talk about it with anyone, and bring the list to our next meeting. **(task)**

6. How to Conduct a Quick Interview with Scaling Questions

An entire meeting can be conducted using only scaling questions. The following two questions are useful when you have a short amount of time with a student and you need to focus on the student's immediate needs. Notice that two different numerical scales are used (adapted from Kral, 1994):

On a scale of 1 to 100, and 100 means that your life is going as best as possible, and 1 means the opposite, where are you today? **(self-concept)**

On a second scale of numbers 1 to 10, and 10 means that you like where you are on the first scale (1 to 100), and 1 means you don't, where would you put yourself? **(self-esteem)**

These two questions are a quick assessment of how a student sees his life (self-concept) and how he feels about his life (self-esteem). A student's two different ratings can give you a quick idea about she feels about her life. For example, a student may rank herself as 40 out of 100 in being happy with her life. On the second scale, she may rate herself as 2 out of 10 on being satisfied with her life.

In this situation, she is likely a customer for change. Another student with the same first rating, may say that he likes being at 40 out of 100. This may indicate that he isn't a customer for change. It could also mean that 40 is the highest he has ever been and he feels good about it. No matter what number they give, you still need to explore their rating:

> *What has helped you get to that number on the scale of 100?*
>
> *When have you been higher? What are the chances of you doing that again?*
>
> *Suppose you move up 10 percent, what would be different?*

7. Assessing Levels of Safety and Suicide Risk

> *On a scale of 1 to 10, and 10 means you will do anything to keep yourself safe, and 1 means you are not sure, where would you put yourself today?*

Everyone should be trained to recognize indicators of suicide and violence and how to take appropriate action. In the following section, I am not suggesting that you disregard the training you have had. The following ideas offer other ways of talking with students at risk.

Traditionally, scaling questions for risk assessment have been framed in a problem-focused way: "On a scale of 1 to 10, 10 means that you are going to kill yourself and 1 means that you aren't sure, where would you put yourself today?"

This question gives you quick feedback about the seriousness of the student's intent. The disadvantage of asking about self-harm in this way is that it is deficit-oriented. Suppose the student says that he is at an 8 on the scale. This gives you information about the seriousness of his intent, but it doesn't allow you room to ask for exceptions or coping strategies. We could ask," When have you been lower on the scale? What will help you move to a 1?" However, in our culture, we usually think of progress as movement towards a higher, not lower number.

A solution-focused scaling question asks about suicidal thoughts in a positive way:

> *On a scale of 1 to 10, 10 means you'll do anything to keep yourself safe , and 1 means that you aren't sure, where would you put yourself today?*
>
> *What has helped you to get to a 2?*
>
> *When have you been higher on the scale?*
>
> *What was helping you cope and keep yourself safe?*
>
> *What will it look like when you move up one notch?*

Notice that the word *safety* is emphasized and that number 1 is vague. We are planting seeds of change by emphasizing safety rather than the thoughts of killing oneself. These series of questions elicit strengths and help to build hope.

After I have asked students or adults these solution-focused questions, they visibly change. They tell me, "When I came to see you, I was at a 2. Now, I am at a 4."

If you are unsure of the student's safety, ask yourself the scaling question:

> *On a scale of 1 to 10, and ten means that*
> *I know she/he will keep her/himself safe,*
> *where would I put the student?*

Pay attention to your intuition. Although a student may tell you that he will keep himself safe, you may notice signs that make you uneasy. Then take all of the necessary precautions.

Case example:
I almost killed myself this week

This case example demonstrates how to use scaling questions to assess for level of risk, to negotiate a safety plan, and help the person generate specific steps towards safety. In this case example, I was seeing Rebecca, a woman in her middle forties, for depression. She lives with her husband and his parents.

Counsellor: How have things been for you in the last two weeks?

Rebecca: Not very good.

Counsellor: What has been happening? You look tired.

Rebecca: Well, I should tell you that I almost killed myself this week.

Counsellor: I'm glad you are telling me this. What happened? **(exploring suicidal thoughts)**

Rebecca: One night, I was lying in the bathtub and I started to think about all of the bad things that have happened to me.

Counsellor: Then what?

Rebecca: Well, I thought about ending it all then and there.

Counsellor: What did you think about? **(exploring plan)**

Rebecca: I thought about slashing my wrists.

Counsellor: But you didn't. How did you manage to overcome the urge to slash your wrists? **(exception- finding)**

Rebecca: I thought of my in-laws.

Counsellor: How did this help?

Rebecca: I knew that they would be the ones to find me.

Counsellor: What made you think that they would be the ones to find you?

Rebecca: Well, they live with us. Because they are elderly, they don't sleep as long as we do, they are often up in the night, and I knew that they would be the first ones to use the bathroom. You see, we only have the one bathroom.

Counsellor: You didn't want them to be the ones to find you. Why not? **(amplifying exceptions)**

Rebecca: Because they are old and they don't need that in their memories. And I do care about them.

Counsellor: You really love and respect them. I'm impressed with how you were able to put aside your memories and the urge to hurt yourself. **(amplifying exceptions)** What else will help you continue to overcome the urge to slash your wrists? **(amplifying)**

Rebecca: I think I need to change my bathtime.

Counsellor: How will that help? **(amplifying her idea for solutions)**

Rebecca: Because right now, I'm at the end of the line, so I can stay in the bathtub for as long as I want and then I mull over these things. If I am in the middle, I know I'll only have half an hour and then it's someone else's turn to use the bathroom.

Counsellor: Makes sense to me. I would never have thought of that. What else will help you to continue to overcome the urge to hurt yourself? **(amplifying change)**

Rebecca: I think I need to see my doctor and to go back on my medication. *(I didn't know that she had gone off her antidepressants)*

Counsellor: How will that help?

Rebecca: I thought I could do without them but they did help.

Counsellor: I agree that it is a good idea to see your doctor, as soon as possible. When can you go to see her?

Rebecca: I thought I would go right after this appointment.

Counsellor: Good. I'll phone the doctor to let her know that you are coming in.

Counsellor: Now, Rebecca, I am still worried about you. On one of those scaling questions, let me ask you a really tough question. On a scale of 1 to 10, 10 means that you will do anything to keep yourself safe, and 1 means that you aren't sure, where are you today? **(assessing level of safety)**

Rebecca: Well, to be honest, when I walked in here, I was at 2 and now I'm at a 4.

Counsellor: What has helped to move it up to a 4?

Rebecca: Just talking about it and knowing that I can keep going.

Counsellor: I'm going to take a think break and then I'll share my ideas with you. You may want to write down what stood out for you in this session.

***

At at the end of the meeting, I complimented Rebecca on her love of her in-laws and on her ideas about what will help her to keep herself safe. I suggested a solution-focused homework task:

> *In the next week, keep track of what helps you continue to overcome the urge to harm yourself and to keep the memories in their place. What you are doing or thinking, and what are other people doing. Write this down and bring it to our next meeting.*

Rebecca saw her physician that afternoon and resumed her medication. During the week, she discovered that she was doing many things to help keep the memories in their place. This helped her not to become overwhelmed by them. She realized that she was most susceptible to them when she was alone and in unstructured time. Changing her bath time was a beautiful solution. Clients come up with solutions that fit for them and with solutions that are far more creative than we could possibly conceive!

SIX

How to Conduct Solution-Focused Meetings

You cannot solve a problem with the same thinking that created it.

Albert Einstein

Y ou have learned about future-oriented questions, exception-finding questions and scaling questions. These can be used in your daily work with students and parents. This chapter describes the framework for how these are used in a solution-focused meeting.

You may have a difficult parent-teacher interview or a special one-to-one meeting with a student. A solution-focused meeting can maximize your effectiveness. A solution-focused meeting is composed of three parts:

> the ***meeting*** itself, when exception-finding and future-oriented questions are asked;

a ***think break,*** when the interviewer takes time to formulate feedback for the student; and

feedback to the student at the end of the meeting.

The Process of a Solution-Focused Meeting

TABLE 6.1 SHOWS THE OVERALL FRAMEWORK of a solution-focused meeting. It is not necessary to rigidly adhere to the framework. Once you are comfortable with the process, you can adjust it to the situation.

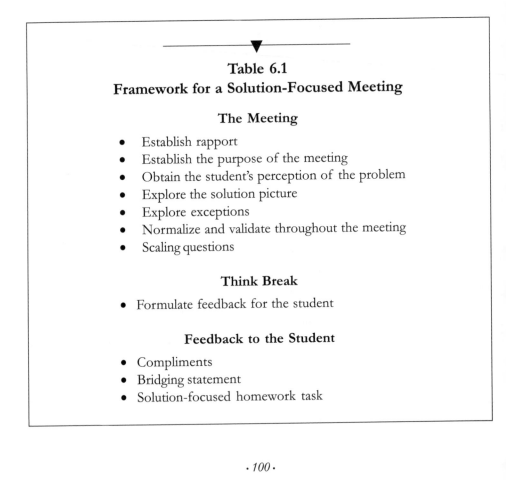

Table 6.1
Framework for a Solution-Focused Meeting

The Meeting

- Establish rapport
- Establish the purpose of the meeting
- Obtain the student's perception of the problem
- Explore the solution picture
- Explore exceptions
- Normalize and validate throughout the meeting
- Scaling questions

Think Break

- Formulate feedback for the student

Feedback to the Student

- Compliments
- Bridging statement
- Solution-focused homework task

The Meeting Process

Establish Rapport

Rapport is important in any context whether we are in a school meeting, a parent-teacher interview, or talking with students. Using the student's language is an effective way of establishing rapport. Listen for key words or phrases the student uses when describing her problem or solution picture. Use these phrases in your paraphrasing statements, in your questions and in your feedback to the student.

Case example:
I want to get my wacky self back

I met with a 14-year old student who was having difficulties both at home and at school. When I asked her the miracle question, she said she would know it happened when she returned to her "wacky self."

Counsellor: How will you know when you have your "wacky self back?

Student: I would be joking with my friends again.

Counsellor: What else would be different?

Student: I'd be going out again and doing fun things with them.

Counsellor: How would your parents know that you got your "wacky self back?"

Student: I wouldn't be staying in my room all the time.

Counsellor: And what would you be doing instead?

Student: I'd be talking with them.

———•———

This student was describing, in her own language, how her self-esteem would be improved. It was much more effective to use her "wacky self" phrase rather than professional jargon regarding self-esteem.

Establish the Purpose of the Meeting

Never assume that you know what a parent or student wants from a meeting. It is helpful to ask goal-setting questions to get a sense of what each party wants. When I meet with parents, I ask:

> *How will you know, by the time you leave my office today, that this meeting was helpful?*

> *How will you know, six months from now, that this meeting was a good idea?*

When consulting with teachers, I might ask:

> *How will you know this consultation was useful?*

> *What will be different as a result of our meeting today?*

Goal-setting questions are very useful in parent-teacher interviews:

> *I have a good idea of what your concerns are. I'd like to ask you a question to help me understand things more clearly. How will you know that this meeting was helpful?*

> *What will be signs to you that this meeting was helpful?*

Obtain the Student's Perception of the Problem

Do not assume that the problem you are concerned about is the problem that the student or parent wants to work on. It is important to find out what they expect of the meeting:

> *How do you make sense of the fact that the teacher sent you to my office?*
>
> *I am worried about how you are doing school. Maybe you have other concerns that I don't know about. What do you think is the problem that needs to be solved?*
>
> *What do you think are the reasons for your son's difficulties in school?*

Explore the Solution Picture

Future-oriented questions invite the student to imagine his future when the problem is solved. The miracle question is a powerful way of asking about the solution picture. Students and parents become very intrigued with this question:

> *Suppose, that after we talk today, you go home tonight, and while you are sleeping, a miracle happens. All of the problems that you are dealing with are solved. How would you know that the miracle happened? What would be the first sign to you that things are different?*

There are many ways to ask future-oriented questions. Younger children may not understand the word *miracle*. Other ways of asking it are:

> *Pretend for a moment that things are better at school. What will it look like when things are better?*
>
> *Pretend your fairy godmother came in the*

*middle of the night and solved all the
problems in school. How could you tell
that she came to your house? What would
be better?*

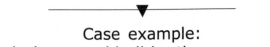

Case example:
the lockers would all be the same colour

A teacher was helping a young boy affected with fetal alcohol syndrome. She asked him to imagine what it would look like when things are better at school. He immediately responded, "The lockers would all be the same colour."

This was his way of telling her that he was overwhelmed by the external stimuli in the hallway. They immediately took steps to simplify his environment. Interestingly, he targeted a solution that is recommended for helping children with fetal alcohol syndrome. In a school with a high percentage of children with fetal alcohol syndrome, the staff removed all the pictures from the hallway walls. This simple step helped the children stay focused.

Explore Exceptions

Sometimes, it is unnecessary to ask future-oriented questions if change is already happening in the present. If the student reports pre-interview change, the remainder of the meeting could focus on building on these changes. If the student is clear about the changes made and is confident that she/he can maintain them, it may not be necessary to ask the miracle question.

In order to focus on strengths, resources and potential solutions, in school case conferences, it is important to ask about exceptions:

When has this student done better?

When is the student more successful?

Normalize and Validate Throughout the Meeting

Using validating statements throughout the meeting creates rapport and a cooperative relationship with the student. Validation means that you acknowledge the student's experience of the situation. It does not necessarily mean that you agree with the student. For example, we can validate a student by saying, "It must be tough to feel that all of the teachers are against you."

Validating statements help to reduce blame and defensiveness. They help to create a non-judgmental atmosphere. Sometimes, parents and students simply need reassurance that they are experiencing normal stages of struggle or change. For example, with parents, it is useful to normalize their teens' rebelliousness as a typical "testing of their wings." A crisis can be normalized as "a time of transition."

It is particularly important to validate a student when he has been involuntarily sent to see you. Validating statements throughout the interview create an atmosphere of respect and rapport.

The following case example shows how validation of the student's resentment, opened the door to solution building.

Case example:
I don't want to be here

Student: I don't want to be here. The teacher thinks I have a problem, but I don't.

Counsellor: Sounds tough. **(validating)** How did you decide to show up, even though you didn't want to be here? **(identifying an exception)**

Student: Because then I'd be in bigger trouble.

Counsellor: So you don't want to be in bigger trouble?

Student: No, I'm in enough trouble already.

Counsellor: *(with humour)* So, you just want medium-sized trouble, not big trouble. **(highlighting resources).**

Student: I guess.

Counsellor: What is it about you that you don't want bigger trouble? Some kids don't care; they just get into bigger trouble.

Student: I never thought about it.

Counsellor: It takes a lot of guts to show up for a meeting that you don't want. And it must be tough to have people telling you what to do. **(validating)**

Student: Yeah.

Counsellor: Knowing that you didn't want to be here and this meeting wasn't your idea, **(validating statements),** how will you know that this meeting will be useful to you? Other people have ideas about what they want you to do here, but I'm wondering what you want? **(goal setting)**

In this interchange with the student, I began by validating his resentment about being involuntarily sent to the meeting. I highlighted that, in spite of this, he showed up for the meeting. While listening to him, I discovered that he is a customer for not getting into bigger trouble. Now, I can begin to help him with his goal.

Scaling Questions

At the end of the first meeting, scaling questions are used to assess the level of the student's motivation to change. This helps you to assess whether you have a visitor, complainant or customer relationship with the student:

> On a scale of 1 to 10, and 10 means that
> you will do anything to solve this problem
> and 1 means the opposite, where are you
> today?

Some students may be very motivated to change, but they may not feel confident that they can change. A second scaling question assesses the student's level of confidence:

> On the same scale, this time, 10 means
> you are very confident you can make
> these changes, and 1 means the opposite,
> where are you today?

A student's sense of progress can also be explored:

> On a scale of 1 to 10, and 10 means that
> the problem that brought you here is
> solved, and 1 means the opposite, where
> are you today?

These scaling questions help to bring the meeting to a close before you take your think break. It is helpful to ask the student:

> Is there anything else you would like to tell
> me before I take a moment to think about
> this?

The Think Break

Formulate Feedback

In the solution-focused model, the interviewer takes a think break at the end of the meeting to formulate feedback for the student. If you are working with a team, this is the time to consult with them. If you are having a one-to-one meeting, with a student or parent, the think break gives you time to wrap up the meeting in a meaningful way. The purpose of the think break is to:

i)   allow you to mentally and emotionally disengage yourself from the interview;

ii) give you time to formulate meaningful feedback for the student; and

iii) create a sense of importance about your feedback.

At the beginning of a meeting, I explain the think break in the following way:

> *After talking with you, I'll take some time*
> *to think about what you have said,*
> *because what you say is important. Then*
> *I'll share my ideas with you.*

This statement conveys my respect for the student's ideas and that the meeting will accomplish something. If I forget to tell the student about the think break, I mention it at the end of the meeting. You need only one or two minutes to formulate meaningful feedback. The think break is a powerful part of the process. It creates suspense and students and parents become very interested in what you are going to say.

If possible, it is helpful to leave the room so that you can emotionally distance yourself from the meeting. I stand in the hallway outside of my office door and jot down my ideas for the message. I also suggest that students and parents use think break time to write down the useful ideas they think came out of the meeting. Some do this, while others simply wait or take a washroom break.

You may not be able to leave the room for your think break. For example, it would not be appropriate to leave young children or a destructive student alone in your office. If it is not possible for you to leave the room, you can turn your chair away or look down while you take a think break.

Some counsellors are reluctant to take the think break because they feel that they are abandoning the student or that it implies that they are not competent. These statements are more reflective of the counsellors' discomfort than the students'. In all my years of counselling, students and parents have never complained about the think break. Usually, they feel good that I am taking time to reflect on what they have said and what will help their situation.

Feedback to the Student

The feedback message to the parent or student is composed of three parts:

> **Compliments** – which highlight the student's strengths and resources

> **Bridging statement** – which links the compliments and the task

> **Solution-focused homework tasks** – to help to sustain the changes initiated in the interview.

Compliments

Compliments highlight the student's resources and create a positive tone for the homework task. When generating compliments for the student, think of two or three things that really impress you. Your compliments must be genuine and sincere. The student or parent is more likely to accept the compliments when you base them on what they did or said during the meeting:

> *I'm impressed with the fact that you showed up today, even though you didn't want to be here.*

*I'm impressed with how you have stuck
with it, in spite of all the difficulties you
have had.*

Bridging Statement

This is simply a transitional statement that makes a link between the compliments and the homework task you are going to suggest. Again, the more you use the student's phrases, the more effective you will be in creating rapport and cooperation. The bridging statement and the compliments help to personalize the homework task and to motivate the student to try out the task:

*Because you said you would do anything
to get off drugs, I'd like to suggest...*

*You were very clear about what it will look
like when things are better. In the next
week...*

*I'm impressed that you showed up today
even though you didn't want to. It is very
clear that you want more freedom and
that you need to convince your teachers
and parents that you can handle it. In the
next week...*

Solution-Focused Homework Task

Solution-focused homework tasks are given at the end of the meeting. The tasks generally fall into two categories: exception-oriented tasks and future-oriented tasks. In exception-oriented tasks, the student keeps track of small signs of improvement. In future-oriented tasks, the student is asked to act as if the changes have already happened.

This chapter has highlighted the stages of a solution-focused interview. You can use the worksheet provided (Table 6.2) as a guideline to structure your meetings. Be sure to maintain rapport in the interview. It is more important to listen to the student or parent than to focus on completing the form. Over time, with practice, these questions will come to you naturally.

▼

Table 6.2
Solution-Focused Meeting Worksheet

Name: _____ Date: _____ Meeting # _____

Type of Meeting: (individual, parent/child, teacher/student) _____

Family Members Present: _____

Others Present in the Meeting: _____

Other Involved Professionals: (ie. teacher aid, pediatrician, probation officer)

_____

1. Current Problem(s): parent, student and teacher's views of the problem

_____

2. Relevant History (ie. medication, learning disabilities, etc.)

_____

3. Solution Picture: Parent, student and teacher's views

_____

4. Exceptions (when are things a little better)

_____

5. Scaling Questions
     Motivation: _____
     Confidence: _____
     Progress: _____

6. Feedback to the Student/Parent
     Compliments _____
     Bridging Statement _____
     Task _____

7. Plans for the Next Meeting _____

SEVEN

How to Put It All Together

In the beginner's mind, there are many possibilities; in the expert's mind there are few.

D.T. Suzuki

Now that you are familiar with how to structure a solution-focused meeting, it is time to reinforce the learning. This chapter outlines the entire process of an actual interview (adapted from McConkey, 1998, reprinted with permission). This is a counselling example. Some of the issues discussed in the meeting would be beyond the mandate of teachers or principals to address. Even if you are not a counsellor, take the time to read this example. It illustrates how solution-focused questions draw out strengths and solutions and what to do when a client or student has unrealistic goals.

Observe how solution-focused questions elicit strengths and the family's ideas regarding solutions. Notice the process of the interview.

▼

Case example:
fighting the "temper monster"

Relevant History

Nine-year-old Christine was having problems with physical aggression at school and at home. She hit and kicked other children, called them names, and was increasingly disruptive in the classroom. The teacher discussed the problems with her mother and recommended counselling.

When Joan called me for an appointment, she explained Christine had a problem with her temper. She explained that the problem had become worse since she and Christine's father had separated. Christine's father, Steve, was also concerned and wanted to attend the meeting. I commended Joan on their willingness to meet, in spite of the recent separation, and set up a time.

Establishing rapport

I spent the first part of the meeting establishing rapport with the family members. In the meeting, there was a great deal of tension and sadness. Joan was close to tears and it was apparent that the separation was not her idea. Christine sat quietly between her parents.

Establishing the purpose of the meeting

Counsellor: *(to parents)* I'm very impressed that both of you have put aside your differences to be here on behalf of your daughter. **(validating)** In order to make the most of this meeting, could you tell me, how will you know this meeting has been helpful to you? How will you know, when you leave today, that coming here was a good idea? **(goal-setting)**

Mother: As I mentioned on the phone, the teacher suggested counselling because of Christine's behaviour in the classroom. She gets a lot of time-outs because she hits kids and calls them names. It's getting so bad that it is interfering with her schoolwork and her friendships with the kids.

Counsellor: *(to father)* Are you concerned about this as well?

Father: Yes. That's why I wanted to attend this meeting, to see what we could do to help Christine.

Mother: It hasn't been easy for her since we've separated. We know that her problems in school are partly related to this. But she can't continue this or she'll get further behind, and it is affecting her relationships with the teacher and the kids. She's always been feisty and now it is worse.

Counsellor: *(to Christine)* Do you agree with your Mom and Dad that this temper has been getting you into trouble at school?

Christine: Yeah.

Counsellor: It sounds like it hasn't been easy for anyone, since your Mom and Dad separated. **(validating)**

My intent in this part of the interview was to highlight the parental strengths, emphasize the parents' commitment to helping their daughter, and begin goal setting. The opening question, "How will you know this meeting has been helpful to you?" is useful for orienting everyone in a meeting towards goal setting.

Validating and normalizing

Counsellor: It sounds like all of you have been through a very difficult time. I'm impressed with how well you *(to the parents)*, have been trying to deal with the separation. It sounds like you know Christine needs to let out her feelings. Sometimes, she just needs to feel sad or angry about it. As you said, it takes time to sort out feelings. Christine, you said it takes time to get used to living in two different houses. All parts of your lives have been changed. And Christine, I'm impressed that you want to make things better at school.

———◦◦◦———

In this interchange, I wanted to validate their experience of the separation process, and highlight their strengths and resources.

———◦◦◦———

Goal setting

Counsellor: I'd like to ask all of you a very unusual question. It will help me understand what you want and how I can help. Suppose that after you leave today and go home, while you are sleeping, a miracle happens. All of the problems that brought you here are solved. The miracle happens while you are asleep, so you don't know it has happened. How would you know when you woke up tomorrow, that the miracle happened? How would you know that the problems were solved?

Christine: *(answering immediately)* Mommy and Daddy would be living together again.

Counsellor: **(validating her)** Of course, you would wish for that. That would be the miracle for you. Now, I'm not sure they will get back together, but suppose they did, what would be different? **(searching for hidden customer needs)**

Christine: Mommy and Daddy would talk nicer to each other. Right now, they yell at each other sometimes.

Counsellor: What else?

Christine: Mommy wouldn't be crying so much.

Counsellor: What would she be doing instead? **(obtaining specific, concrete indicators of the solution picture)**

Christine: She'd be playing with us more, and going out more.

Counsellor: What would be different, after the miracle, about all these problems you have been having in school?

Christine: They'd be gone!

Counsellor: Really! How?

Christine: I would just go to school. Right now, I'm taking my feelings out on them.

Christine was really in touch with everyone's feelings. The *miracle* discussion took about twenty minutes. The parents listened intently to Christine's description of the miracle picture. This question gave her permission to express her needs and concerns, and it became clear that she wanted her parents to talk more cooperatively with each other, and for her mother to feel better. I was not sure that the parents were willing to attempt reconciliation and I assessed the possibility of this with a scaling question.

Using scaling questions to define achievable, solvable goals

Counsellor: Christine, I'm going to ask you a very tough question. Let's say, on a scale of 1 to 10, 10 means the chances are high that your Mom and Dad will get back together, and 1 means you know in your heart, that they won't get back together, where do you think it is today?

Christine: *(somberly)* It's at a 1.

Counsellor: How do you know that for sure?

Christine: Because they've already signed the papers.

Counsellor: I see. Of course, you would wish they would get back together **(validating)**, but in your heart, you know they won't.

Counsellor: *(to parents)* Do you agree with Christine that the chances of you getting together again are at a 1?

Father: Yes.

Mother: I think we could work it out, but he doesn't.

Father: We've tried many times, and I'm not willing to go through that again.

Counsellor: I'd be willing to meet with the two of you separately to explore all of the possibilities.

Father: I'm willing to attend meetings for Christine, but not for the two of us. It's too painful and I don't want to go through it again.

Counsellor: *(turning to the mother)* It's clear you are in a great deal of pain regarding the separation. Christine is very much in tune with your feelings. Would you be interested in meeting me by yourself for one meeting?

Mother: Yes, I'd like to do that.

Counsellor: We'll set a time at the end of the meeting.

Counsellor: *(to father)* I appreciate that you were honest with your daughter and me. In the future, should you want to set up a meeting, just let me know.

Counsellor: Of course, Christine would wish that you would get back together. I'm impressed with how you listened and allowed her to talk about how hard it has been for her.

Counsellor: *(to Christine)* Knowing they aren't going to get back together, what pieces of your miracle picture can you still keep? **(negotiating achievable goals)** You have really good ideas of what your mom and dad can do to make it easier for you.

Before the meeting ended, I knew that I had to address the parents' worries about Christine's school problems. The next excerpt shows how I addressed Christine's behaviour difficulties in a positive and fun way.

Externalizing the problem

The externalization technique helps to separate the problem from the person (White, 1986). Chapter 11 gives more details about how teachers can use this technique in the classroom, and Chapter 12 discusses how to use this technique in anger management groups for children and adolescents.

Notice how I talk with Christine as if the temper problem is a person or thing separate from her. This creates some distance between her and her behaviour and helps her to develop a sense of personal mastery over the problem.

Counsellor: Tell me more about this temper that gets you into trouble. Where does it start in your body? **(beginning to externalize the problem as separate from her)**

Christine: *(pointing to her right temple)* It starts right here in my head! It goes down my neck and into my arm, and makes me punch kids!

Counsellor: This sounds like a big temper monster! Then where does it go?

Christine: It goes down my body and out my leg and makes me kick kids.

Counsellor: Oh, this is a really big temper monster! Does it sometimes go down your neck and out your tongue and make you say bad things?

Christine: Oh yeah!

Searching for exceptions

Counsellor: Have there been times when you stood up to the temper monster? When could it have got past your neck but you stopped it?

Christine: That's easy, I've been really trying in the past two weeks, but no one noticed. I had only one time-out last week.

Counsellor: Really! How did you do that?

Christine: I just told it to go away.

Counsellor: Just like that?

Christine: Yes!

Scaling questions to assess student confidence to change

Counsellor: You must be very strong. When you make up your mind to do something, you just do it. Now I'm going to ask you another number's question. This time, 10 means you're really confident you can keep standing up to the temper monster, and 1 means you're not confident. Where are you today? Do you know what confident means?

Christine: Yes, confident means I know I can do it. I'm at an 8. I know I can do it.

Counsellor: Wow, that's really high! What will help you move to a 9 on that scale?

Christine: My cat, because it's going to bite the monster's head off!

Counsellor: Of course! Why didn't I think of that! Will you draw a picture of how your cat will help you?

While Christine drew her picture, I talked with the parents about how they could build on Christine's ideas and make the divorce process go as smoothly as possible. After Christine completed her picture, I told her that I could make copies of it on the Xerox machine. I asked, "How many copies would you like to have?" She wanted one copy for her desk, one in the time-out area and one at each of her parents' homes to help her "fight off the temper monster."

Taking a Think Break

Counsellor: I'm going to take a moment to think about what you all have said. You have many good ideas about what will help to make things better. I'm going to leave my office for a moment, and then I will share my ideas with you. You may want to write down the good ideas that you remember, in case I forget some.

I then left my office and stood in the hallway to think about what compliments and homework task that I wanted to give to the family. The think break gives me time to formulate meaningful feedback to the family and it heightens the impact of the feedback, because the family is in a state of anticipation, wondering what I am going to say.

Feedback to the Family: Compliments

Counsellor: As I said earlier, I am very impressed that the two of you have come together, as parents, to help your daughter, in spite of the discomfort and pain still present. I am impressed that you *(father)* wanted to be at this meeting, and that you *(mother)* invited him to be here. This is a very clear sign of you both trying to handle the divorce in the best way possible. You obviously love your daughter very much.

Christine, you are very much in touch with your parents' feelings. You know how hard this divorce has been for all of you. It's important that you, as parents, allow Christine to share how she feels about the divorce. Christine, you had really good ideas about what will make it easier. You said it would be easier if Mom and Dad would talk nicer to each other, and that your temper won't even bother you in school.

Bridging Statement

Christine, I'm amazed at how you've been fighting off the temper monster in the last two weeks, and how confident you are that you can keep fighting it off. Eight out of ten is really high in confidence! I have some ideas to help with the temper that has been getting you into trouble.

Solution-Focused Homework Task

To help you keep this up, I want you to keep track, every day, of how many times you stand up to the temper monster. Times when it could have taken over, but you didn't let it. Write down these times and then talk about it with your Mom and Dad. And I'd like both of you, to keep track of how many times Christine overcomes the urge to lose her temper. When she could have said something bad or hit someone, but she didn't.

Christine's parents liked the homework task and decided they would each set up a star sheet for at home and at school, to keep track of when she was doing well. At the end of the meeting, I set an appointment to meet with Joan by herself.

This case example shows the process of a solution-focused interview. As you can see, the miracle question freed Christine to talk about what she needed from her parents to help her deal with divorce process. An important part of this interview was the use of scaling questions to negotiate achievable goals with Christine and her parents

The parents were motivated to make some changes in how they dealt with each other. It was clear that the parents were supportive of Christine and allowed her to express her feelings about the divorce. Because they were supportive, I felt comfortable shifting to Christine's temper problem. If the parents had minimized the impact of the separation on Christine, or if they were unresponsive to her sadness, I would have asked Christine more solution-focused questions about how they could help her.

Two weeks later, I met with Joan for an individual session. She reported that Christine's behaviour had improved dramatically at home and school. I saw Joan for four more sessions, to support her in the divorce process.

How To Deal With Setbacks

Eight months later, Joan requested another meeting because Christine's temper problem was re-occurring. When setbacks occur, it is helpful to reassure students, parents and teachers, that setbacks are a normal part of progress. Change is often a process of two steps forward and one back, as the student moves toward change. When dealing with setbacks, often students just need to be reminded of their previous solutions.

In the meeting, we discussed some of the divorce tensions that had returned and I normalized this process. I noted that she had done well for eight months and we reviewed some of the strategies that had helped Christine before this setback. After reviewing them, she was confident that she could keep on track.

EIGHT

How to Keep Change Going with Solution-Focused Homework Tasks

In the next week, keep track of when things are better.
Come back and tell me what you found out.

(Berg & Miller, 1992)

S olution-focused tasks are like icing on a cake. They are the final touches that help to sustain the changes initiated in the meeting, and to orient the student, teacher or parent toward solutions after the meeting.

How you use solution-focused tasks depends on your role in the situation. A teacher can give a task to both a student and herself:

Let's keep track of what helps you in class.

The teacher may give herself the task. A counsellor or principal may suggest the same task when a teacher asks them for assistance regarding a student.

In his book, *Keys to Solutions* (1985), de Shazer describes solution-focused tasks as "skeleton keys." Just as skeleton keys are used to open any type of lock, solution-focused tasks can unlock change with any type of problem.

His team first experimented with the first session formula task, which was designed to help clients become clearer on their goals for counselling:

> *Between now and the next time we meet, observe what is happening in your life (marriage, relationship, school) that you want to continue to have happen (de Shazer, 1985, p.137).*

The team discovered that not only did clients become clearer about their goals, the observation task helped clients create changes in their life. Clients became more focused on solutions rather than problems.

These end-of-session tasks are described as *formula tasks* because they help to unlock change, no matter what the problem is. As you will see, the tasks are open-ended. The student or parent fills in the solution picture with what is meaningful to them. When you suggest a homework task, it is important to tailor the task to the student or parent's situation with compliments and the bridging statement.

How to Use Solution-Focused Homework Tasks with Students and Parents

SOLUTION-FOCUSED TASKS ORIENT US TOWARD exceptions and focus the student, parent or teacher on what is already working. The tasks are also useful for creating exceptions or desired behaviours when the student or parent seems unable to find any positives. Finally, they help the student to sustain changes between meetings. Solution-focused tasks fall into one of the three following categories:

Exception-oriented tasks. These are designed to orient the student (parent, teacher) towards exceptions. Often, these are observation tasks in which the person is asked to keep track of when things are better.

Future-oriented tasks. In these tasks, the student is asked to act as if the solution picture has happened.

Creating exceptions or change. Tasks such as "do something different," and the "surprise task" prompt the initiation of new behaviour.

Table 8.1 lists the tasks that I most frequently use (adapted from de Shazer, 1985; Berg & Miller, 1992; O'Hanlon & Weiner-Davis, 1989). The tasks can be used with students, parents, groups, and in consultations with teachers or principals. Many tasks are based having the person do more of what works.

When deciding on which task to use, consider the type of working relationship you have with the person. If you are unsure whether you have a customer relationship, it is useful to proceed conservatively, and give the person an observation task rather than an action task. In a visitor relationship (see Chapter Nine), the person is given a thinking task or perhaps no task at all. The next section explores how these eight types of tasks can be applied in a variety of situations and different problems.

▼

Table 8.1
Types of Solution-Focused Tasks

Exception-Oriented Tasks

Keep Track of When Things Are Better
Keep track of when things are going better in your life (in school, at home). What are you doing? What is your family (friends, teachers) doing?

Amplifying Pre- Interview Change
Many times, people notice in between the time they make the appointment for counselling, and the first session, that things already seem different. What have you noticed about your situation?

First Session Formula Task
Between now and the next time we meet, observe what is happening in your life (marriage, family) that you want to continue to have happen, no matter how small. Write it down and bring your list to our next meeting.

Pay Attention to When you Overcome the Urge to...
Pay attention to when you overcome the urge to skip school (binge, drink, use drugs, lose your temper). Come back to the next meeting and tell me what you find out.

Future-Oriented Tasks

Pretend a Miracle Has Happened
Take two days in the next week, and pretend a miracle has happened. Don't tell anyone, and notice what difference it makes in your life. Come back and tell me about it.

(Table 8.1 continued on next page)

Coin Toss

Every morning, toss a coin. If you get a head, that's the day you pretend a miracle has happened. Do everything that you would do on a miracle day. If you get a tail, do everything you would do on a normal day. Pay attention to what is different on the miracle days.

Creating Exceptions or Change

Do Something Different

Between now and the next time we meet, I suggest that you do something different, no matter how strange or weird, or off the wall it may seem. The only important thing is that whatever you decide, you need to do something different. Keep track of the difference it makes.

Surprise Task

Do at least one or two things that will surprise your teacher (parents, friends). Don't tell them what it is. Parent (teacher) your job is see if you can tell what it is that she is doing.

Eight Types of Solution-Focused Tasks

1. Keep Track of When Things are Better

> *Keep track of when things are better in your life (in the classroom, with your family, in school). What is different at these times? What are you doing? What are your parents (friends, teacher) doing?*

This is a wonderful non-threatening task, which orients people towards exceptions. When students, teachers, or parents are experiencing problems, they are so immersed in the problem picture that they do not notice exceptions. It is important to validate the person's struggles and to use a bridging statement so that the task makes sense to the person. Here is how I framed the task when I consulted to a teacher:

> *It sounds like a frustrating time for you.*
> ***(validation)*** *In order to help me get an*
> *assessment of the situation **(bridging***
> ***statement)**, could you keep track of*
> *times when the student is doing a little bit*
> *better? What is he doing? What are you*
> *doing? What are the other students doing?*
> *Anything that is helping in those moments,*
> *write them down and bring them to our*
> *meeting. This will help me to help you.*

The teacher would have been offended if I simply asked her to be more positive with the student. In this message, I emphasized that the teacher's observations will help me with my assessment, and hopefully, it orients her towards exceptions.

2. Amplifying Pre-Interview Change

> *Many times people notice in between the*
> *call for an appointment and the first*
> *meeting, that things already seem*
> *different. What have you noticed that is*
> *different about your situation since you*
> *asked for this appointment?*

Chapter Two discussed the phenomenon of pre-treatment change. Use this question at the beginning of the first interview when a parent or student has asked for the appointment. Some agencies give this task on the telephone when a client calls for a first appointment. After obtaining the necessary information, the receptionist tells the client:

In order to help your counsellor help you as best as possible, keep track of when things are better between now and when you come in for your first meeting. Write down anything that is a little bit better and bring this list to your meeting with the counsellor.

School counsellors may not have a receptionist or scheduled appointments. In that case, you can devise a solution-focused pre-interview worksheet (see Table 8.2). Students can complete it while they are waiting for their meeting with you. With this worksheet, you can get students to think of solutions before they see you. It is also useful to give this worksheet to parents and teachers before an important meeting. It orients everyone towards exceptions and goal setting.

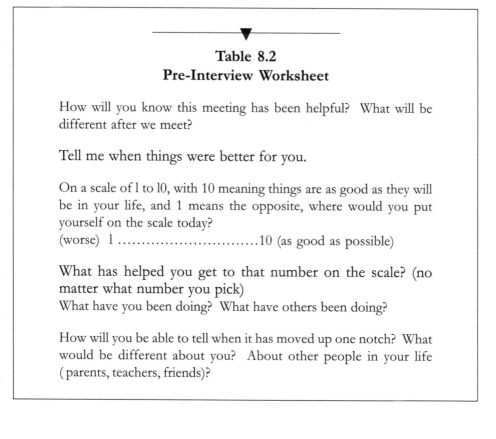

Table 8.2
Pre-Interview Worksheet

How will you know this meeting has been helpful? What will be different after we meet?

Tell me when things were better for you.

On a scale of 1 to 10, with 10 meaning things are as good as they will be in your life, and 1 means the opposite, where would you put yourself on the scale today?
(worse) 1 ....10 (as good as possible)

What has helped you get to that number on the scale? (no matter what number you pick)
What have you been doing? What have others been doing?

How will you be able to tell when it has moved up one notch? What would be different about you? About other people in your life (parents, teachers, friends)?

3. The First Session Formula Task

> *Between now and the next time we meet,*
> *observe what is happening in your life*
> *(school, classroom,) that you want to*
> *continue to have happen. Write these*
> *things down and bring your list to the next*
> *meeting.*

This task is one of the easiest to begin using. I frequently give this task to workshop participants so they can experience the effect of a solution-focused task. I ask them to discuss with a partner, "What is happening in your life that you want to continue to have happen, no matter how small? Small things such as cuddling with your children, talking with a friend or reading a good book." Participants report that while the task seems so simple it has great impact. It helps to clarify what is important in life, to set priorities, and to remember to feel grateful for what one has. Those who have a difficult time thinking of positives in their life become determined to make some changes in their life.

4. "Keep Track of When You Overcome the Urge To..."

> *Pay attention when you overcome the*
> *urge to skip school (drink too much, lose*
> *your temper, binge). Write down what is*
> *happening at those times and bring the list*
> *to our next meeting.*

This is one of my favourite tasks because it is so versatile, simple and effective. This task is useful with children, youth and adults for a wide range of problems. For example, I have used the task to help students overcome the urge to run away, use drugs, lose their temper, smoke cigarettes, or harm themselves. It can be used with eating disorders. "Keep track of when you overcome the urge to binge or to purge."

The word *when* implies change will occur and directs the student's attention to exceptions. This task is more useful when the student is a customer for changing her behaviour in some way. A student who is a visitor may not be ready to do the task if she doesn't believe her behaviour is a problem.

You can give this task to significant others in the student's life, such as parents and or teachers. When the student knows that other people are watching for changes, the student is more motivated to make changes in her behaviour. Involving others helps to expand the solution picture, and orients everyone towards looking for exceptions.

5. Pretend Tasks

> *Pick two days in the next week, and
> pretend that the miracle has happened.
> Act as if it has happened, and notice
> what's different on those days.*

This task helps to artificially introduce exceptions. Children love the playfulness of *pretending*. One young girl asked me if she could pretend that things were better every day, so she could really fool her parents! Teenagers like the pretend task because it helps them to save face. Of course, once they begin to pretend that things are better, change begins to happen. The wording of the task varies according to the situation and type of problem. Here are some alternate phrasings:

> *Pick two days in the next week, and
> pretend that you like school. Don't tell
> anyone and write down what's different on
> those days. What's different about the
> teachers, your parents, or you. Bring your
> list to our next meeting.*

> *This week, whenever you do math, just
> pretend that you like it. See what
> happens.*

Pick two times this week and pretend that you feel confident. Write down what's different at those times.

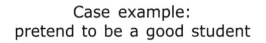

Case example:
pretend to be a good student

A Grade 10 student was brought to counselling by her mother. Her grades were dropping, she skipped classes, and as a result, both her parents and her teachers "were on her case." Although she wasn't sure she wanted to do better in school, it was clear she was a customer for getting her parents and the teachers "off her back."

In our conversation, I discovered that she was a drama student. I explored at length what characters she had played and how she put herself into the role of a character. She agreed that it took a lot of skill and imagination on her part to be able to play different characters.

I asked how she would play the character of a good student. She stated that the character would attend school regularly, "suck up" to the teachers and act interested in school and do homework. I asked her if she was up to playing this difficult role. Suppose she took this role, what difference might it make in her life? She was intrigued.

I suggested that, in the next week, she pick two days and pretend to be a good student and act the role as if she were in a play. I emphasized this was an experiment, so she shouldn't tell anyone that she was acting. I asked her to write down what was different on the days she was pretending. I wished her luck in playing this difficult part.

One week later, she reported that things went more smoothly with her parents and teachers on the days she was *acting* the role of a good student. I encouraged her to continue acting in the next two weeks. Later, as she became proficient in this role, I gave her a new challenge.

When using the pretend task with young children, the wording may need to be adjusted to the their developmental level:

> *Pick a day as your special day and that is the day you act like when things are better. Do what you would on a good day and notice what is different on those days.*

> *This week, take two days and pretend that school is going better. Notice what is better on these days. Don't tell me which days you pick. I'm going to guess which days you picked. We will talk about it at the end of this week.*

When consulting with teachers, I have suggested this variation:

> *Pick two days in the next week and pretend to like the student who is most frustrating to you. Tell yourself on that day, that this is the day you will pretend to like the student. Write down what's different on those days, about you, the student and the class.*

In my workshops, teachers laugh when I give this example but they get the point. There are times when they feel so frustrated with a student that they are focused only on the negatives. This task helps them to back up and change their reaction to the student. If that doesn't work, then we look at other strategies.

6. Coin Toss

> *Every morning, flip a coin. If you get a head, that's the day you pretend a miracle happened. Do everything that you would do on a miracle day. If you get a tail, do everything you would do on a normal day. Pay attention to what is different on the miracle days. Write down what you notice and bring your notes to the next meeting.*

This is another fun task that intrigues students. Flipping a coin introduces the possibility of exceptions. When the coin turns up *a head* the student acts out the miracle picture on that day. Remind the student to notice what is different on those days, and to write this down for the next meeting. This helps to amplify exceptions. If the coin shows *a tail* the student is asked to carry on as normal. The *tail* picture is left vague so the student will pay more attention to the *head* picture.

The task playfully gets students and parents to change their behavior. Here are other examples of how to use this task to help students.

Lack of confidence

> *On the day you get a head, that's the day you pretend to feel confident. If you get a tail, just carry on as normal. Notice what is different on the days you get a head. Write this down and bring your list to the next meeting.*

Problem of depression

> *When the coin comes up with a head, that's the day you pretend to feel happy. Notice what is different on those days.*

Self-esteem problems

On the day the coin shows a head, that's the day you pretend to feel good about yourself. Notice what is different on those days. Tell me what you find out.

Substance abuse problems

When you get heads that's the day you act as if the miracle has happened. That's when you are staying away from the crowd, overcoming the urges and doing other parts of the miracle picture. On the days that you get tails, carry on as normal.

School problems

On the days that you get heads, those are the days that you pretend to be a good student. Notice what is different on these days.

Students are intrigued with the coin toss task because it involves an element of surprise. Many students I have worked with were so excited to try out a *head* day, that when the coin showed *tail* they pretended it came up as *head*!

7. Do Something Different

Between now and the next time we meet, I suggest that you do something different, no matter how strange or weird, or off the wall it may seem. The only important thing is that whatever you decide, you need to do something different. Keep track of the difference it makes.

This task is useful when a student, parent or teacher is caught in a repetitive problem pattern. For example, parents may lecture or yell at their teenager, the teen becomes increasingly rebellious, and the pattern escalates.

Selekman (1992) uses this task in his solution-focused parenting groups, to help parents change their reaction to their teen's problem behaviour. One mother's teen-age son was verbally abusive towards her. Her usual reaction was to pleadingly ask him what she did to deserve such treatment. When this didn't work, she would dissolve into tears.

After the group session, she decided to try something different. Whenever her son was verbally abusive, she started to do crazy things, such as jumping jacks, or reciting nursery rhymes. He was taken by surprise and never knew what she was going to do next. This task allowed her to gain some control in the situation and to playfully change her reaction to her son. Some teens were so happy with the change in their parents, they asked to attend a meeting!

You can suggest this task to teachers to help them unlock power struggles with students. Linda Metcalf (1995) tells how a teacher changed her reaction to a defiant student. The student arrived late for class with a note from the office. When the teacher asked for the note, the student angrily chewed it up and spit it on the floor. The teacher calmly picked up the note, told the student that she couldn't read it and asked the student to get another one.

8. Surprise Task

Do at least one or two things in the next week that will surprise your teacher (parents, children). Don't tell them and notice what difference it makes.

This task is another fun way to interrupt problem patterns. When you work with students, ask them to try this out as an experiment and report to you what they learned. If you want to amplify the task further, ask the teacher or parent to guess what the small surprises are, and keep a list of them. This helps everyone shift to a positive lens.

Solution-focused tasks amplify changes that are elicited and built during the interview. Most students, teachers or parents are willing to do these simple observation tasks. It is important to tailor the task to the person with compliments and the bridging statement. Remember, if you are unsure whether you have a customer relationship, don't push for change too quickly. Chapter Nine gives you strategies for working with students who are in a visitor relationship.

▼

Part Three
Facing Tough Problems

NINE

How to Work With Difficult Students

I don't have a problem. The teacher thinks I have a problem.

O ne of the more challenging tasks that principals and counsellors face is how to be solution-focused with students who have been sent to their office by someone else. Usually, a frustrated teacher or parent sends a student to your office with the request that you "do something with this student." Often, the individual sending the student is frustrated and may feel that she/he has already bent over backwards for the student.

In these situations, the referring person is in a complainant relationship with you, focused on how the student should change. Complainants want change to happen but are not ready to look at how they may be part of the problem or part of the solution.

Furthermore, the student may also be in a complainant relationship with you: "My teachers are jerks." "My parents are the problem." Or the student may be a visitor: "I don't know why I'm here. The teacher sent me. I don't have a problem, the teacher thinks I have a problem." The student has not requested the meeting, and feels resentful for being sent against her/his will.

How can you be solution-focused when a student doesn't want your help? The first section of this chapter discusses useful strategies for working with difficult students. The second section describes how to work with students who are visitors. These students, initially, do not seem to have a goal or a problem that they would like your assistance with. They are "involuntary clients." The third section outlines strategies for working with students who blame others for their problems.

I would like to add a word of caution. I have used the word "difficult" simply to describe problem scenarios that students and teachers face. It is important to remember that all students have strengths and resources. Furthermore, problem behaviour makes sense when it is understood in its context. Many of these students may be struggling with issues in other parts of their life, and these difficulties become translated into behaviour problems at school.

Strategies for Working with Difficult Students

WHEN YOU WORK WITH STUDENTS WHO are "involuntary clients", it is helpful when the roles of the school professionals are clearly delineated (Walter & Peller, 1992). The administrator should assume the *social control* role and enforce the school consequences for misbehaviour. The counselling process should be non-judgmental and non-punitive. If counsellors are asked to assign consequences to a student, this puts both the counsellor and student in a bind. The student may perceive the counsellor as an authority figure instead of a confidante.

If you are an administrator and you are taking both the counselling and social control roles, this can be a difficult balance. You can balance these roles by establishing a solution-focused tone in the school, and by having a good relationship with students. When a student is sent to your office, you can engage the student in thinking about solutions as well as consequences.

First, when working with these students, it is important to listen for the *hidden customer*. For example, a student might declare that he just wants "the teachers to back off." It is crucial to elicit and negotiate goals that are relevant to the student.

Secondly, it is important to involve the referring person in a way that orients her/him to look for exceptions. Students frequently complain that when they do make changes, their teacher or parents do not notice. Consequently, the student loses motivation to keep trying.

When a Student is an Involuntary Client

When a student is sent for counselling, she/he may blame others for his problems. "I didn't ask for this meeting. The teacher sent me here. I didn't want to be here." In these situations, it is important to validate and acknowledge the student's anger or resentment for being sent to you.

Your first step is to merge with the student. Think of a merging lane in traffic. We merge with the traffic flow and then we change lanes or make a turn in another direction. Similarly, we need to first merge with the student. Too often, we make the mistake of being directive and insist that the student change lanes because that is the direction we think he should take. The student then becomes more angry and resistant.

Use the following key principles (Table 9.1) when working with students who have been sent to your office. In the case examples, notice how the interviewer proceeds slowly and doesn't confront or push for change.

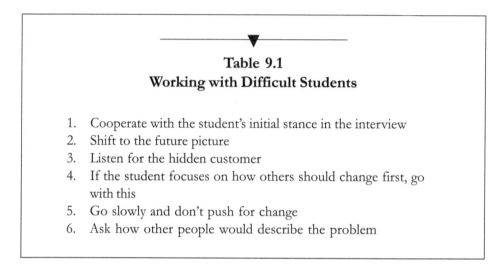

Table 9.1
Working with Difficult Students

1. Cooperate with the student's initial stance in the interview
2. Shift to the future picture
3. Listen for the hidden customer
4. If the student focuses on how others should change first, go with this
5. Go slowly and don't push for change
6. Ask how other people would describe the problem

Case example:
I don't have a dope problem

A teacher sent a high school student to the counsellor's office because she was concerned about the student's dropping grades. The teacher suspects the student has come to class high on marijuana, and that this is affecting the student's academic work.

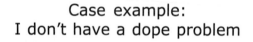

Asking how other people would describe the problem

Counsellor: Thanks for coming in today. How do you make sense of the fact that the teacher sent you to my office? **(inviting the student to share her opinion)**

Student: I don't know *(defensively)*. You're the one that kids get sent to if they are in some kind of trouble.

Counsellor: Sometimes, but that's not the only reason. *(persisting)*

So, how do you make sense of the fact that the teacher asked me to see you?

Student: She thinks that I'm not doing the best I can in school. I'm doing all right.

Counsellor: What do you suppose gives her the idea that you aren't doing as best as you could? **(asking how the teacher would describe the problem)**

Student: She thinks that just because I had better grades last year, I should get them this year. She doesn't realize that school is tougher now that I'm in a higher grade.

Counsellor: Sounds like school has been tough for you. I get the sense that the teacher believes in you and has seen you do better. **(amplifying exceptions)**

Student: Yeah, I guess so.

Goal-setting with scaling questions

Counsellor: I'm going to ask a strange question, to help me understand how to make the most of this meeting with you. After all, you didn't ask for this meeting, and yet you showed up, so I want to make the most of your time here. **(validating)** On a scale of 1 to 10, and 10 stands for school is going as best as possible, where would you put it today?

Student: I'd say an 8.

Counsellor: Okay. What makes you say an 8? **(cooperating with the student's stance instead of confronting her that this is an inflated number)**

Student: Well, I'm showing up for classes. That's more than you can say about some of the other students.

Counsellor: True. What helps you to get to school, to keep showing up? **(exploring exceptions)**

Student: My friends are here. We like to hang out together.

Counsellor: Anything else that helps you to get to an 8?
(cooperating with the student's stance)

Student: My marks are all right. I'm not failing any of my subjects.

Asking how others would rank the problem on the scale

Counsellor: Okay. Suppose your teacher was here right now, and I asked her the same question. Where do you think she would put it on the scale? **(asking how the teacher would rate it)**

Student: Huh! She would put it at a 2.

Counsellor: And on that same scale, where do you think your parents would put you today? **(asking how her parents would rate it)**

Student: They would say the same thing as the teacher. They're always on my case these days.

Counsellor: What do you suppose the teacher and your parents see that makes them lower on the scale than you? **(asking how others see the problem)**

Student: They think that I smoke too much dope.

Counsellor: What gives them that impression?

Student: *(frustrated)* Ask them!

Counsellor: Sounds like you would really like to have them off your case. **(hidden customer)**

Student: You bet!

Asking how others would describe the solution picture

Counsellor: Suppose they were here, what would they say they would notice when it moves up one notch on the scale? **(asking how others would describe signs of solutions)**

Student: Well, I guess they would say that I wouldn't be stoned at school.

Counsellor: How would that help? **(amplifying potential solutions)**

Student: They think that I can think more clearly when I'm not stoned.

Counsellor: What do you think? Are you able to concentrate clearly when you are stoned? **(moving slowly and remaining non-judgmental)**

Student: Are you crazy? Where have you been? We get stoned to feel good, not to think more clearly.

Counsellor: Oh, so it is harder to concentrate on schoolwork when you are stoned. Suppose that you don't come to class stoned, what difference will that make in getting your parents and teachers off your back? **(amplifying change)**

Student: You don't understand. I hang out with my friends at lunch hour and that's when they like to smoke. I don't get to see them after school because we get on a different school bus right after school. **(hidden customer)**

Counsellor: Right, your friends are important too. Sounds like you have a dilemma. **(validating).**

Listening for hidden customer goals

Counsellor: Sounds like you would really like to have your parents and teachers off your case. **(focusing on hidden customer goals)** What will it take to move up just one notch on the scale?

Student: Maybe I'll just have to smoke with my friends on the weekend.

Counsellor: How will that help?

Student: The teacher and my parents will get off my case, for one thing.

Counsellor: How else will it help not to smoke at lunch hour?

Student: In the afternoon, I'll be in a better space. The teacher says that I'm behind and that she's willing to take some time at lunch hour to help me to catch up.

Counsellor: What does she see that makes her believe in you, and go the extra mile to help? **(amplifying exceptions)**

Student: *(thoughtfully)* I don't know. I didn't think about it.

Counsellor: Obviously, there is something about you that gives her high hopes for you and your future. What is it you want for your future? Any idea of what you want to do with your future? **(searching for hidden customer goals)**

Student: Not really. But I do want to finish high school and I want a good job. **(hidden customer goals)**

Turning a visitor into a customer for change

Counsellor: So what will it take, starting tomorrow and for the next week, to convince your parents and your teacher that it is moving up one notch on the scale? **(asking how others would describe signs of solutions)**

Student: I can't be stoned at school.

Counsellor: Sounds like a good plan. What will you tell your friends?

Student: That we'll have a good time on the weekend but I can't smoke at school.

Counsellor: That's gutsy of you. True friends will stand by you and not give you a hard time. True friends will help make your dreams about finishing school and getting a good job come true. **(planting seeds of change)**

Student: I never thought about it that way.

Counsellor: It's just a thought. **(wondering out loud)**

Feedback and solution-focused task

Counsellor: I'm impressed with many things that you have said and done. First of all, you showed up for this meeting even when you didn't want to be here. It is clear to me that your parents and teachers believe in you. Furthermore, you said that you want to finish school and to have a good job. You must believe in yourself too. **(compliments)**

You also said that when you smoke at lunch hour it's hard to concentrate in class and you get further behind. And then you're in trouble at school and at home. And yet, you want to keep your friends. I thought you had a good idea about how to balance these things out, by smoking only on the weekends. **(bridging statements)**

In the next week, keep track of what helps you to overcome the urge to smoke at lunch hour, what you are doing and what your friends are doing. And notice what difference it makes not to be stoned at school. Notice what is different about your teacher, your parents and you. Write these things down and bring the list to our next meeting. It's a personal experiment that you are going to try out, so for now don't tell anyone about it. **(task)**

It was important to focus on a goal that was meaningful to the student. Initially, she was not a customer for giving up marijuana. However, she was a customer for getting her teachers and her parents "off her back." Therefore, she was willing to modify the time and place of her use of marijuana towards meeting this goal. The solution-focused task simply amplified her ideas for change.

Wonder out loud about the possible consequences of not changing

If the student in this case example remained in a visitor relationship about changing her behaviour, the message would be different.

Counsellor: I'm impressed that you came to this meeting even though it wasn't your idea and you didn't want to be here. It sounds like your teacher and your parents really believe in you. You said that you want to finish school and have a good job, so you must believe in yourself too. (**compliments**)

It sounds like you have a dilemma. On the one hand, you want to visit with your friends at lunch hour and you want to keep them. On the other hand, you said that when you smoke dope at lunch hour, you are less alert in school and get further behind. This gets you in more trouble in school and with your parents. And it doesn't help you to finish school so that you can have a good job. (**validating her dilemma**)

I'm wondering whom you want to have in charge of your life? Do you want your friends to be in charge of your life or do you want to be in charge of your life? Do you want marijuana to be in charge or do you want to be in charge? (**wondering out loud about consequences**)

Counsellor: You're in a tough spot. Think about it and come back to see me one more time. **(going slowly)**

When working with visitors, it is important to give compliments and validate the student's dilemma. Don't push for change too quickly. Visitors aren't ready for action tasks. Ask them to think about it and come back for one more meeting. This decreases the potential for resistance, because there is nothing for the student to resist against. In this case scenario, the student is likely to return after this feedback because she knows that she won't be lectured or confronted. If the problem persists, then she will then face more consequences. The administrator should handle the consequences while the counsellor helps the student deal with her problems.

When a Student Blames Others for Her or His Problem

Case example:
the teacher is a jerk

This case example shows how to work with a student when he blames someone else for his problems and initially, takes no responsibility for the problem or solutions. Notice how the counsellor acknowledges and validates the student's anger. When the student feels heard and understood, he is more likely to participate in the interview.

Counsellor: How do you make sense of the fact that the teacher sent you to my office? **(eliciting his opinion)**

Student: I don't know. The teacher is a jerk.

Counsellor: Things don't sound like they are so great for you in the class. **(validating)**

Student: You could say that.

Counsellor: Obviously, coming to my office wasn't your idea. **(validating)**

Student: You got that right.

Counsellor: And coming to my office probably isn't your idea of having a good time. **(validating)**

Student: You bet.

———•———

Shifting to the future picture

When working with resistant students, it is helpful to quickly shift to the future-oriented questions. These help to draw out the hidden customer, something that is important to the student.

———•———

Counsellor: Knowing you don't want to be here, and knowing this isn't your idea of fun, how will you know that this meeting has been helpful to you? **(future picture)**

Student: The teacher will get off my back. **(hidden customer)**

Counsellor: Of course. **(validation)** Suppose things are better between you and your teacher, what will that look like? How will you know when things are a little bit better? **(future-question)**

Student: The teacher would back off.

Merging with the student's focus on how others should change first

When asked to describe the solution picture, a student may focus on how other people will change first. This is a natural reaction because it is easier to visualize change by thinking about how other people will be different. For example, try this on yourself: Suppose, your family life is going as smoothly as possible, what will that look like? What will be happening? What else will it look like?

What did you begin to think about in your solution picture? Most likely, you first thought about how your children, spouse, or other household members would change. We don't think about how we will change first.

Similarly, when the student talks about how others should change first, merge with this stance. At least the student is talking about change. Too often, teachers and counsellors confront students too quickly.

––––•◦•––––

Counsellor: And what will your teacher do instead? **(focusing on what will be different)**

Student: She would crack a smile at me once in a while

Counsellor: Suppose she did that, what difference would it make for you? **(solution-building)**

Student: She's such a grouch, it would make her class more bearable.

Counsellor: What else will be different when things are better? **(amplifying the solution picture)**

Counsellor: She would notice that I'm not the only troublemaker in the class. Other kids make trouble too.

Counsellor: So she would spread trouble around? **(use of humour)**

Student: Yeah. *(surprised)*

Counsellor: Okay. What else will it look like **when** things are better?

Student: She would notice that I am trying sometimes.

Counsellor: Suppose she did notice when you are trying, what difference would that make for you?

Student: I would feel like trying more often.

Counsellor: Of course. What else would you notice when things are better?

Student: She would help me once in a while. I don't understand half of that stuff. But I don't want to ask questions. I don't want to look stupid in front of my friends. **(hidden customer)**

Counsellor: Suppose she helped you without your friends knowing, what would that look like?

Student: Maybe I could give her a secret signal.

Counsellor: That's a great idea.

Counsellor: You have really good ideas of what it will look like when things are better. The teacher will smile at you once in a while she will notice when you are smiling; and she will help you when you give a secret signal.

———◆———

In this conversation, the student has focused on how the

teacher will change first. He was in a complainant relationship and the counsellor cooperated with his stance. As the interview progressed, it became clear that he is a hidden customer for getting the teacher "off his back" and for getting assistance without it being obvious to his friends. He remains focused on how his teacher should change, but the solution-building process has begun (Figure 9.1).

Figure 9.1

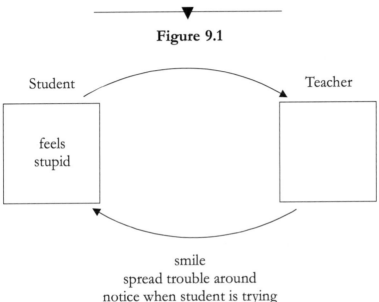

The next section shows how to shift the discussion to include the student's ideas about how he will change.

Asking how the teacher would notice changes in him

Counsellor: When *(not if)* these things are going on and the teacher is doing all of these things, what will be different about you?

Suppose the teacher is sitting here with us right now, what would she say would be different about you when things are better?

Student: She would say that I would show up for class more often.

Counsellor: Suppose you did show up for class more often, how would that be helpful?

Student: She would get off my case.

Counsellor: Right. What else? (amplifying)

Student: She would see that I would do my homework.

Counsellor: Suppose you did your homework, how would that help?

Student: I wouldn't be so far behind.

Counsellor: That makes sense. What else?

Student: I wouldn't be in trouble at home for my marks.

Counsellor: So your parents would get off your case.

Student: Yeah.

———•———

The student is now more willing to think about how he will change his behaviour. When the counsellor asked how the teacher would notice signs of change, this allowed him to save face. He wasn't ready to say, "I know I have to change too." Figure 9.2 shows how the solution pattern has been completed.

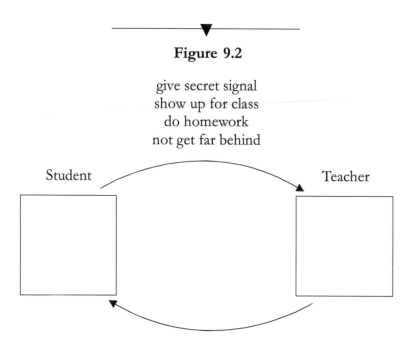

Figure 9.2

give secret signal
show up for class
do homework
not get far behind

Student   Teacher

When you are working with students who have been involuntarily sent to you, the think break and feedback at the end of
the meeting are a crucial part of the interview process. The
student certainly doesn't expect compliments and the feedback amplifies the progress made in the meeting.

Feedback to the Student

Counsellor: I am impressed that you showed up for this meeting
even though it wasn't your idea and even though you didn't want
to be here. It's pretty clear that you would like to have the teacher
back off. You have great ideas of what it will look like when
things are better. You said the teacher would be smiling more, she
would notice when you are trying, and that she would help you
when you give a secret signal. I will mention to the teacher that you
will be giving her an idea for a secret signal. **(compliments)**

You have good ideas about what the teacher will notice when

things are better. You would show up for class more often and this would help you to not get so far behind. **(bridging statement)**

This week, keep track of when things are better between you and the teacher. Write down what is different at those times. What you are doing and what the teacher is doing. Don't tell anybody what you are doing; it's your own experiment. Come back and tell me what you have found out. **(task)**

The student is likely to follow through on the task because the counsellor built on his ideas for the solution picture and his goal for getting the teacher to back off.

Orienting the Referring Person to Solutions

In this case example, if the teacher is in a customer relationship, the counsellor could suggest the same solution-focused task to the teacher:

> *Keep track of when things are better with this student.*

If the teacher is a complainant, the teacher may not be willing to do a task. The message to the teacher who is in a complainant relationship might sound like this:

> *I've met with the student you sent to my office. It sounds like things have become quite frustrating with this student.*
> ***(validating)*** *We talked and it's clear that he would like to have things go better for him in class. His main concern is that he doesn't want to look stupid in front of his friends. He is going to give you a secret signal for when he needs help.* ***(ideas for specific strategies)***

I don't think he has noticed all things you have done to try to help him. **(bridging statement)** *I have asked him to keep track of times when things are better in class, what he is doing, and what you are doing to make things better. He's going to bring his list to the next meeting with me.*

This message validates the teacher's struggles with the student and gives her ideas for new strategies. Furthermore, she is told that the student is making a list of when things are better in class. When she knows the student is making a list, hopefully, this will motivate her to be more solution-oriented with the student.

Solution-Focused Referral Sheets

You can orient a teacher or parent towards solutions with a solution-focused referral sheet (Tables 9.2 and 9.3). When a teacher or parent completes the sheet, they will begin to think about resources, strengths and goals instead of dwelling on the history of the problem and on deficits.

▼

Table 9.2
Solution-Focused Parent Referral Sheet

Dear Parent(s), thank you for taking the time to complete this sheet. It will help me to help your child.

Name of Student _____ Grade _____ Date _____

Your Name _____ Phone No. (H)_____ (W)_____

Your Relationship to the Student _____

1. What are your concerns? _____

_____

2. What have you tried so far? What has helped? _____

_____

3. What are your child's strengths, hobbies, and interests? What motivates her/him?

_____

4. When have things been better? (small things or times when things are a little better) _____

_____

5. On a scale of 1 to10, and 10 means that your child is doing as best as possible, and 1 means the opposite, what number is it today? _____

6. How will you know it has moved up one notch on the scale? What will your child be doing? What else will help? _____

_____

_____
Parent Signature

▼

Table 9.3
Solution-Focused Teacher Referral Form

Dear Colleague, thank you for taking the time to complete this sheet. It will help me when I meet with the student.

Name of Student _____ Grade _____ Date _____

Your Name _____ School _____

Phone _____

1. What are your concerns? _____

_____

2. What have you tried so far? What has helped a little? _____

_____

3. Please list the times when you notice the student is doing well. This will give us clues to solutions. Please be as specific as possible. For example, "She focused on her work for 10 minutes and tuned out the other students." "He kept his temper in check." _____

_____

_____

4. On a scale of 1 to10, and 10 means the student is doing as best as possible, and 1 means the opposite, what number would you give the student?_____

5. How will you know when the student has moved up one notch on the scale? What will the student be doing? What else will help? _____

_____

_____
Teacher Signature

TEN

Solution-Focused Strategies for Principals

The way leaders conceptualize the purpose of their organization determines how their organization will run.
(Phillip Schlechty, Schools for the 21st Century)

The solution-focused model can transform the culture of your school. One principal noticed a decrease in the number of students sent to his office for discipline issues, after teachers were taught solution-focused strategies. Now, whenever this principal changes schools, he ensures that his staff receives training in this model. Other principals find the model invaluable for defusing meetings with angry parents.

This chapter focuses on how principals (and other members of the administrative team) can use solution-focused strategies to:

1. Discipline students

2. Deal with problem students
3. Deal with bullying problems
4. Do solution-focused team building

Solution-Focused Discipline Meetings With Students

As NOTED IN THE PREVIOUS CHAPTER, IF YOU are an administrator, and you are taking both the counselling and social control roles, this can be a difficult balance. When discussing solutions and consequences with students, one admininstrator nicely balances these two roles by saying:

> *I wear two hats. One is the school principal hat. That's the hat that says no matter what, when certain things happen, like someone gets hurt or property is destroyed, there are consequences that are here for everyone.*
>
> *The other hat helps me make school go better for students. That's the hat I'm going to put on now. Suppose school is going as best as possible for you, what will that look like? What will we be doing? What will you be doing? What will be happening when things are a little better?*

After they discuss the solution-picture, he involves the students in determining the appropriate consequences:

> *What will it take to convince the teacher that you are serious about turning this problem around?*
>
> *What consequences do you think need to*

*happen to show other people that you are
taking this seriously?*

*What will it take to convince other
students (parents, teachers) that you are
getting back on track?*

School principals can make a positive difference with students who are sent
to their office for discipline problems. One school principal shared the following
example of how she now deals with problems in a solution-focused way.

When you read the transcript, notice how she defuses their defensiveness by
asking about the problem "from the teacher's perspective." Also, notice how
quickly she moves to the solution picture.

Case example:
do something with these students!

A grade two teacher had sent two students to the office because
of their disruptive behaviour in the classroom. They were
standing on their desks, talking out loud, and generally not
paying attention. The principal met the children in the reception
area, shook their hands, asked their names, and escorted them
into her office.

Principal: Can you tell me why you were sent to my office? *(in non-
threatening tone of voice)*

Students: I don't know. *(apprehensively)*

Principal: Suppose the teacher was here. What do you think she
would say? **(asking about how the teacher would describe the
problem)**

Students: She would say that we were doing bad things.

Principal: Like what?

Students: Like standing on our desks.

Principal: What else would she say?

Students: She would say that we were talking out loud, and that we weren't listening.

Principal: You have good ideas of what made the teacher ask you to come to my office. **(compliments)**

Shifting to the future

Principal: I'm going to ask you a crazy question. When you go back to the classroom, suppose things are better between you and the teacher. What would that look like? How could the teacher tell that things were better? **(asking how the teacher would notice changes)**

Students: Well, we wouldn't be standing on our desks.

Principal: What would you be doing instead? **(getting specific indicators of change)**

Students: We would be sitting at our desks.

Principal: What else would be better? **(amplifying the solution picture)**

Students: We wouldn't be talking out loud.

Principal: What would you be doing instead?

Students: We would put up our hands if we had a question.

Principal: What else would it look like when things are better?

Student: It would be so good she wouldn't even know we were there!

Principal: That would be amazing! Suppose you started to do all of these things, sitting at your desks, putting up your hands, what would be different about the teacher?

Students: She wouldn't be yelling at us.

Principal: What would she be doing instead?

Students: She would be nicer to us.

Principal: What else would be better?

Students: She would let us be one of the helpers. **(hidden customer)**

The principal used many strategies to skillfully engage the students' cooperation. First, she created rapport by shaking their hands and treating them respectfully. Next, she tried to get their understanding of why they were sent to the office. When they said they didn't know, she didn't confront them. Instead, she asked how the teacher would describe the problem. This strategy allowed the students to save face and helped to get information about the problem. She then shifted to the solution picture, by asking how the teacher will notice when things are better. This is a non-confrontational approach that helps students to describe a solution picture (Figure 10.1). When students generate solutions, they are more likely to follow through on them.

The principal then capitalized on the students' ideas for change with a solution-focused task.

Figure 10.1

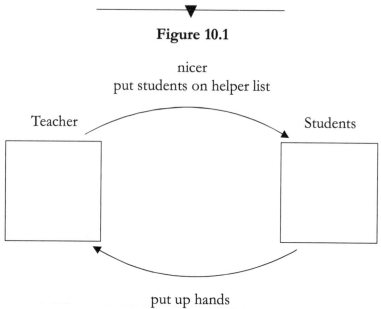

nicer
put students on helper list

Teacher   Students

put up hands
sitting on chairs
listening

Solution-focused task

Principal: You have great ideas about how things will look when things are better between you and the teacher. **(compliments)** Let's try something out.

Students: Okay.

Principal: **(solution-focused task)** When you go back to class, I'd like you to do all of the things that you said would make things better with the teacher. Like sitting at your desks, putting up your hands, and paying attention. Let's see if she can catch you at them. *(making the task playful)* She has to guess when you are doing these good things. I'm going to let her know that we talked and that you are going to surprise her. Just try it out for today and see what happens. *(making the task manageable)*

Involving the teacher in the solution-focused task

During recess, the principal talked with the teacher about the meeting with the students. Notice how she validates the teacher's frustration before making any suggestions.

———•———

Principal: I've talked with the students. They are very clear about why they were sent to the office. **(validating the teacher's concerns)**

Teacher: Good.

Principal: They had good ideas about what they need to do to make things better. They said they will put up their hands before asking questions, sit on their chairs, and will pay attention. **(building on the teacher's goals for sending the students to the office)** I'm sure you have told them this before, but it's important because they came up with these solutions

Principal: I've asked them to try to do these things and told them that you would try to catch them at it. **(bridging statement)** Whenever you notice them doing anything positive, just give them a little signal. Say something such as "I saw that" in a playful tone, and carry on with your teaching. **(focusing on exceptions)** They're motivated right now and this will help.

Teacher: Sure.

———•———

The solution-focused task oriented both the students and the teacher towards exceptions. Prior to learning the solution-focused model, the principal stated she would have been more confrontational. "You must have some idea about why you are here." She then would have lectured the students about the rules of appropriate conduct. She liked the fact that this meeting was less confrontational and the students generated the solutions.

When a Problem Student is Transferred to Your School

THE PERFECT TIME TO CONDUCT A SOLUTION-FOCUSED meeting is *before* the transferred student is integrated into a classroom. It is crucial to involve the student and the parents in goal setting, and to highlight the student's strengths. This sets a positive, collaborative tone for the school year. The following case example shows what a difference a solution-focused meeting can make.

▼

Case example: a 10 percent average

Child Welfare placed Sandy, a thirteen-year-old girl, in a foster home because of family difficulties. At the end of the first semester of grade eight, her average was only 10 percent. Sandy was transferred to a different school for the second semester, with the hope that this would give her a fresh start. Sandy and her foster mother attended a meeting with the principal of the new school before she entered the program.

Principal: *(after establishing some rapport)* I understand that you are hoping to have a fresh start at this school. **(positive goal)**

Student: *(cautiously)* Yeah.

Principal: Suppose this school is going really well for you, what will that look like? **(goal setting)**

Student: Well, I'd be in some courses that I really like.

Principal: What kinds of things interest you?

Student: I like acting.

Principal: We have a great drama teacher here, and I'll introduce you to her. What else will it look like when school is going well?

Student: I wouldn't be kicked out.

Principal: Sure. **(validation)**

Principal: How about your marks? Do you want to pass the year?

Student: Yeah, but why try? You know that my marks were really bad in my last school.

Principal: Just suppose for a moment that things are going better in this school. What mark do you think you could get at the end of the school year? **(goal setting)**

Student: I could pass.

Principal: What mark could you get?

Student: I could get 50 percent. But why try? I'll still flunk the year because of my marks at my old school.

Principal: If you get 50 percent, that's a huge improvement from 10 percent. When you get 50 percent in our school, I'll consider that you have passed the year. I could work it out that your average from last semester wouldn't affect your mark here. Is that a deal?

Student: *(surprised)* Yeah!

Principal: When has school been better for you? **(exception finding)**

Student: I was doing better before all my family stuff started to happen.

Principal: You know what you need to do to make things better.

Student: Yeah.

Principal: I'm going to take you at your word that you will bring your mark up to 50 percent. **(bridging statement)** I'd like you to keep track of when things are better this week and write them down. **(task)** Notice what your teachers are doing to make things better, what you are doing, or what your foster mother is doing to help. Notice anything that helps to make things better. Your teachers and I will also keep track of what's helping to make things better. Let's meet in a week to compare our lists.

At the end of the school year, the student's average was 72 percent! The child welfare worker was so astounded by her progress, that she requested the school records before she was convinced that the student had indeed improved.

Dealing With Bullying

WHEN A STUDENT HAS BEEN THREATENED OR BULLIED, you will first ask reportive questions to find out what happened. These questions (see Chapter One) are used to get the history of a problem and to track the problem pattern. After you have enough information about the problem, you can then shift to using solution-focused questions.

In a bullying situation, it may not be appropriate to talk with both students together, as the victim may feel intimidated and fearful in the presence of the other student.

Interview with the Victim

When you meet with the student who has been victimized, solution-focused questions are invaluable for drawing out his ideas for solutions. This process in itself is empowering.

> *Suppose things are better, what will that look like? What will the other student be doing? What will we be doing? What will you (your parents, friends,) be doing when things are better?* **(goal setting)**

Scaling questions help you and the student to concretely assess the level of safety the victim feels:

> *On a scale of 1 to 10, 10 means that you feel safe, and 1 means that you don't, where would you put it today? What has helped to get it to that number?*
>
> *When have you felt safer?* **(assessing level of safety)**
>
> *What number does it have to be at for you to feel safe? What will be happening to help?* **(establishing safety plan)**

Interview with the Bully

When I meet with these students, I listen for strengths, resources and the *hidden customer*. Bullying behaviour may be a reflection of many different problems. In younger children, bullying behaviour may simply reflect a lack of social skills. These children want to have friends, but simply do not know how to go about it.

Bullying may be an indicator of serious, underlying issues in the student's life, such as child abuse or family violence. These situations are more than simply school issues and the appropriate resources need to be put in place.

For some teens, who are dealing with multiple problems in their lives, aggression can be an act of desperation. Chapter 12 describes how a solution-focused program helped students who had been suspended for aggressive and violent behavior.

Solution-focused questions help to draw out the *hidden customer*. Students will disclose what is bothering them because the questions are non-threatening:

*How do you make sense of what happened today? **(inviting his opinion)***

*Suppose the other student(s) were here, what would he say happened? **(asking how the victim would describe the problem)***

*When have things been better for you in school (at home, making friends)? **(exception finding)***

*Suppose things are better for you in school (at home, making friends), what will that look like? **(goal setting)***

Suppose the other student was here, what would he say it will look like when things are better?

What would he see that is different about you?

What would the other students (teachers, parents) see when this problem is solved?

What will it take to convince the student (teachers, parents) that you are turning things around?

What will it take to convince them that they are safe around you?

Once you have engaged the student in the interview, scaling questions are extremely useful for assessing if the student is ready to make some changes. It is important to keep a respectful, non-judgmental tone of voice:

> *On a scale of 1 to 10, and 10 means that you will do anything to make things better, and 1 means you aren't sure, where would you put yourself today?* **(assessing motivation)**

> *On the same scale, 10 means that you will do anything to make things safe for the other student, and 1 means the opposite, where would you put yourself on the scale?* **(assessing level of safety)**

> *What will it take to convince the other student (us, your parents, your friends) that you are serious about making things better and safer for everyone?* **(asking how others would rank their safety level)**

The solution-focused approach holds students accountable for generating solutions – this automatically focuses them on how they will change their behaviour. Likewise, when the student is involved in generating ideas for consequences, the discipline process becomes more meaningful.

Solution-Focused Team Building

TABLE 10.1 GIVES SOLUTION-FOCUSED GUIDELINES to help you remain solution-focused when you work with your staff or when you consult with teachers.

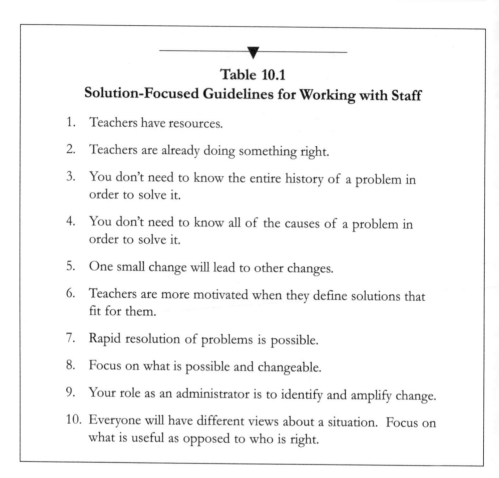

Table 10.1

Solution-Focused Guidelines for Working with Staff

1. Teachers have resources.

2. Teachers are already doing something right.

3. You don't need to know the entire history of a problem in order to solve it.

4. You don't need to know all of the causes of a problem in order to solve it.

5. One small change will lead to other changes.

6. Teachers are more motivated when they define solutions that fit for them.

7. Rapid resolution of problems is possible.

8. Focus on what is possible and changeable.

9. Your role as an administrator is to identify and amplify change.

10. Everyone will have different views about a situation. Focus on what is useful as opposed to who is right.

The next section shows how you can put these guidelines into action. It describes how to use solution-focused questions with a school staff group to help them resolve conflicts.

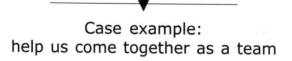

Case example:
help us come together as a team

Judy, a school principal, asked me to facilitate a team-building session with her staff. She had been with the school for one year and was concerned that the teachers were split into two groups. Half of the teachers had been with the previous administrator, and the other half was new to the school.

Conflicts had developed because of different expectations, of the principal, regarding discipline. The *old* staff members were frustrated because she didn't instill fear when they sent disruptive students to her office. They liked the authoritative style of the previous administrator. Instead, the new principal incorporated counselling strategies before taking a hard line with students. She believed the problems were not simply behavioural problems, but a reflection of family and community problems.

Judy's goals, for the day, were for me to teach solution-focused concepts to the staff, and facilitate a team-building discussion that would help them resolve their conflicts. I cautioned her that these were large goals. Judy hoped, at least, to get the process started so they could continue it.

On the day of the meeting, I made it clear to the staff that I would not be taking anyone's side in the discussion. Rather, my role was to facilitate the meeting and help them to generate solutions. I told them I would pose some solution-focused questions for them to discuss in small groups, and then they would share their ideas with the whole group. I emphasized their ideas would be typed out and all would get copies.

To begin, I asked them to form small groups with *old* and *new* staff members. I requested that each group designate a group recorder and a group reporter. The group recorder was responsible for writing the group's ideas on flip chart paper, and the group reporter would share their ideas with the large group. The first question I asked them to discuss was an exception- finding question:

What is happening in your classes and in your school that you want to continue to have happen? Think about small, daily things. What are teachers doing? Parents doing? Administration doing? Students doing?

As the small groups discussed this question, the atmosphere became more relaxed. Group members made comments such as: "It's more fun to come to work when there is humour." "The students pay more attention when I make the classroom fun." "Things go better in the classroom when I am rested."

Overall, the small groups focused on positive things such the use of humour among staff, collaboration, respectful behaviour between staff and students, and consistency in enforcing school rules. After the whole group sharing, several staff remarked that there were more positive things happening than they had realized.

I felt that the team building process was on the right track and I introduced a goal setting question:

Suppose there was a miracle, and all of the problems regarding the discipline policy are solved? What will that look like? What will teachers be doing? What will students, parent and administration be doing when the problems are solved?

After I introduced the miracle question, I emphasized the importance of describing the solution picture in terms of "what will be happening" as opposed to "what won't be happening." As I walked around the room, I heard some staff begin to vent and describe the miracle picture by saying, "this won't be happening." Their colleagues gently reminded them to think about "what will be happening instead?"

After the small groups discussed the miracle picture, the group reporters shared their group's ideas. Signs of the miracle picture were: "We'll smile at one another." "I'll feel good about coming to work." "We'll back each other up." "Expectations regarding discipline will be more clear." "We'll be consistent. If pushing and shoving in the hallway is not acceptable, then we will all deal with it." They described all of the small things that would help to make their daily lives go more smoothly. At this point, there was a lot of animated energy in the room.

The staff also described how parents and students would be involved in formulating the discipline policy, that parents would support teachers, and that parents and students would have a clear understanding of school expectations.

The whole group discussion then shifted to the role of the administrator. Some teachers were outspoken about the fact that "when I send a child to the office, it is for a reason and the administrator should back me up no matter what." Other teachers responded that it wasn't fair to expect this of her because she knew more about family issues that might be contributing to the student's problems. This discussion was important. The administrator found it helpful to hear the teachers' ideas about solutions without the pressure to justify her position.

These first two questions took up most of the morning. After lunch, I wanted to shift the discussion to a plan for action. Again, I wanted to highlight their resources and strengths and used a scaling question to help them assess their level of progress and to set goals.

> *On a scale of 1 to 10, and 10 means that you have a discipline policy, which you can all live with, and 1 means the opposite, where would you put it today?*

What has helped to get it to that number?

Most participants gave ratings between 4 and 6 on the scale. When asked about what has helped them to get that number, they identified many factors. "The fact that we are having this meeting is progress." "We already have a good discipline policy in place, we just need to clarify some areas." In the whole group sharing, many staff stated they were surprised at the consistency in the ratings. Many expressed surprise that they were doing better than they thought!

In the final part of the solution building process, I wanted to ensure that the staff had some concrete ideas and strategies they could begin to implement immediately. During the breaks, several staff told me they hoped that a concrete plan would be developed. They were frustrated that previous staff development days had focused on brainstorming ideas with little follow through.

The group was ready for the next question:

What will it look like when it moves up one notch, starting tomorrow morning? What will be signs that things are better?

After small group discussions, the whole group quickly narrowed down the areas they wanted to focus on. First, they decided to organize a discipline policy committee with representatives from all of the key stakeholder groups. Second, they believed it was important to rename the policy with a more positive name such as *Signs of Respect*. Third, in the next staff meeting, they wanted to discuss guidelines for how to handle students' pushing and shoving behaviour in the hallways. This was the area with the least consistency among the staff members.

At the end of the day, many teachers commented they liked the positive focus of the model. Some later attended my workshops to learn how to use the model with students and parents. The administrator was pleased with the results of the day. As part of the follow-up, I sent her a typed summary of the flip chart notes for distribution among the participants. In a follow-up phone call, she indicated that they were continuing their work on the discipline policy.

When you use solution-focused questions to facilitate a staff meeting, it is important to be open-minded. Be genuinely interested and curious about the ideas that group members generate. If the staff senses you have a hidden agenda, you will lose their trust. A trusting atmosphere is crucial for solution building.

ELEVEN

Solution-Focused Strategies for Teachers

Every student is capable of learning. There are no failures, only discouraged learners.

Teachers want to be positive with their students, but on a bad day, it can be hard to remain positive. This chapter gives you solution-focused strategies for the classroom and for working with difficult students and parents. We will discuss how you can:

1. Reframe problem behaviour
2. Search for islands of competence
3. Use indirect compliments
4. Use goal-setting questions
5. Conduct solution-focused parent-teacher interviews
6. Use scaling questions to develop individual program plans (IPP)
7. Do solution-focused conflict resolution.

Seven Solution-Focused Strategies for Teachers

1. Reframing: Changing from a Negative to a Positive Frame

When we label students as difficult, troublemakers, or learning disabled, we limit our ability to see their strengths and resources. Diagnoses and labels may be necessary, but if not carefully used they can be like barbed wire; we can get caught on them (Metcalf, 1999).

Reframing means changing the way you view a student's problem behaviour. It is non-productive to see these students as failures. It is more helpful to think of them as *discouraged learners*.

Reframing is a tool that will help you to develop cooperation with students. By changing your view of problem behaviour, you will be less reactive and more proactive. Table 11.1 gives examples of how you can change the meaning of problem behaviour from a negative frame to a positive frame. This is more than just playing with words. Once you positively reframe how you think or feel about a student's behaviour, your tone of voice and your reactions will be different.

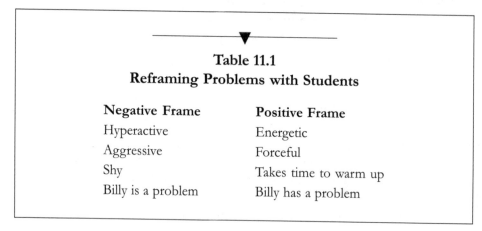

Table 11.1
Reframing Problems with Students

Negative Frame	Positive Frame
Hyperactive	Energetic
Aggressive	Forceful
Shy	Takes time to warm up
Billy is a problem	Billy has a problem

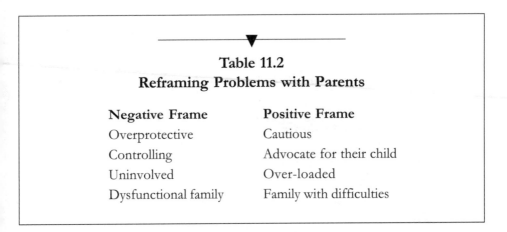

Table 11.2
Reframing Problems with Parents

Negative Frame	Positive Frame
Overprotective	Cautious
Controlling	Advocate for their child
Uninvolved	Over-loaded
Dysfunctional family	Family with difficulties

When you reframe problem behaviour, it is helpful to think about the positive intent behind the student's, or parent's behaviour, or the positive effect of the behaviour. For example, when I work with young children who bully other children, I ask them what they are hoping to achieve. Often, the student says he wants to have friends. The positive intent behind the bullying behaviour is an attempt to get friends. He is just going about it in unhelpful, misguided ways.

Table 11.3 describes a useful practice activity for developing skills in reframing problems (adapted from Molnar and Lindquist, 1989).

2. Search for Islands of Competence

When we search for exceptions, we are looking for small islands of competence. If you have a problem student, it is helpful to look for *anything* that is going well with the student and for times when the problem behaviour is less frequent. Often, this search can unlock clues to solutions.

It is easier to assist a student when you work from a focus on strengths rather than a focus on deficits. With some students, you may need to highlight any strength that they demonstrate, even if these are not directly related to their academic performance.

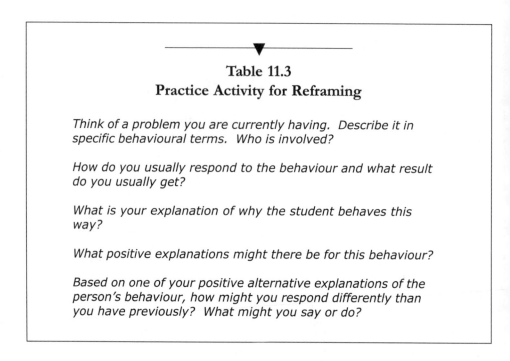

Table 11.3
Practice Activity for Reframing

Think of a problem you are currently having. Describe it in specific behavioural terms. Who is involved?

How do you usually respond to the behaviour and what result do you usually get?

What is your explanation of why the student behaves this way?

What positive explanations might there be for this behaviour?

Based on one of your positive alternative explanations of the person's behaviour, how might you respond differently than you have previously? What might you say or do?

The following case example shows how school staff developed a more cooperative relationship with difficult parents by focusing on exceptions to the problem.

Case example: parents who refused to attend parent-teacher interviews

A school had many students with behaviour and learning difficulties. Often, when teachers called the parents of these high-needs students to discuss their child's problems, the calls were not returned. Also, it seemed impossible to get parents to the school for a meeting. Needless to say, this was very discouraging for everyone involved.

Initially, the teachers labelled these parents as *resistant*. Then, they decided to look at the situation through the eyes of the parents. The teachers realized, that for many of the parents, a phone call from school meant just one more complaint about their child, or one more instance when their child was failing. Furthermore, many of these parents had their own history of negative childhood experiences in school.

The staff brainstormed ideas about how to turn the situation around. One idea involved changing how they used the telephone. They decided to use their phone calls to highlight exceptions. When a classroom teacher noticed that a child was doing well, she called the parents to let them know about positives, without placing any expectations on the parents. "I thought that you might want to know that Jenny was really cooperating today." "Bobby really paid attention when we were doing spelling."

As a result of this experiment, many of the problem parents became more cooperative. Highlighting exceptions on the telephone was one step towards developing a cooperative relationship with them.

3. Use Indirect Compliments to Amplify Change

The solution-focused model makes a distinction between direct compliments and indirect compliments (DeJong & Berg, 1998, p.32). Direct compliments come to us naturally. "Good for you!" "I'm proud of you!" Some students do not respond to praise. Indirect compliments are questions that draw out competencies from the student. They direct the student's attention to something he is doing that is useful. Indirect compliments help to promote self-esteem and a sense of personal mastery. Use indirect compliments to amplify exceptions:

> *How did you figure out that math problem?*
>
> *How did you manage to hit the wall instead of one of the other students? You were so angry and yet you made sure you didn't hurt anyone.*
>
> *How do you keep coming to school even though you don't like it?*

One elementary teacher reports that these questions helped her to promote a positive and effective classroom environment (Osenton & Chang, 1999). Furthermore, the keener students noticed when she was using indirect compliments and began to use them with each other!

4. Goal-Setting Questions

When students are involved in setting goals and generating solutions, they are more likely to internalize and follow through with them. The next example describes how a grade one teacher used solution-focused questions with her class to generate rules of appropriate conduct.

Case example:
the solution-focused classroom

In the beginning of the school year, the teacher usually told her students about the rules for appropriate conduct. After learning the solution-focused model, she decided to involve the students in generating these ideas.

Teacher: Children, let's talk about what will make this class go as best as it can. How will we know when the noise level is too much and how will we know when the noise level is just right? **(goal setting)**

Students: We won't be yelling.

Teacher: What will you be doing instead? **(presence of desired behaviour)**

Students: We'll listen to you.

Teacher: How will I know when you are listening to me?

Student: We'll look at you when you talk.

Teacher: Right! What else will it look like when the class is going just right? **(staying in the solution picture)**

Student: We'll have fun.

Teacher: Yes, when it goes well, we'll all have fun being here.

Teacher: What else will help to make it go well? **(searching for more concrete indicators of the solution picture)**

Student: We won't hit each other.

Teacher: What will you do instead?

Student: We'll tell you if someone is bugging us.

Teacher: Yes, then we can talk about how to solve the problem.

Teacher: Let's pretend that there is a fly on the wall. What would that little fly see when our class is going smoothly? **(asking how someone else would describe the solution picture)**

The children went on to describe more indicators of appropriate behaviour. She recorded their ideas on flip chart paper and posted them on the walls. She told them that they would have fun catching each other doing these things and that she would be watching for these things as well. Each week she reviewed with them what went well, and they added to their list.

5. Solution-Focused Parent-Teacher Meetings

Some parent-teacher meetings can be very tense. A parent, who is upset, may vent about what the teacher and the school have done wrong. Some teachers take the comments personally and react defensively. It is hard to remain impartial and professional when someone is verbally attacking you. When you work with someone who is that angry, shift the meeting from the problem picture to the future solution picture:

*Obviously, you want things to be better for your child and so do I. **(validating the parent)** In order to make the most of this meeting, I'm going to ask you an unusual question. **(bridging statement)***

*How will you know, by the time you leave here today, that this meeting has been helpful?**(shifting to the future)***

*When things are better, what will your son be doing? What will I be doing? What will you be doing? **(including all the stakeholders in the solution picture)***

Use the worksheet in Table 11.4 to guide your meetings. When you begin the meeting, be sure to take some time to establish rapport and to highlight positives about the student. You can give the worksheet to parents and students for them to complete and bring to the special meeting. This will help to orient everyone towards thinking about solutions

▼

Table 11.4
Solution-Focused Worksheet for
Parent-Teacher Meetings

Student Name _____ Parent's names _____ Date _____

Number of Meetings _____ Present at the Meeting _____

Why are we here? What are our concerns? What is the problem?
Parent(s) _____
Student _____
Teacher _____

When has the student been doing better?
Parent(s) _____
Student _____
Teacher _____

Suppose the problems that brought us to this meeting are solved, what will that look like?
Parent(s) _____
Student _____
Teacher _____

On a scale of 1 to 10, and 10 stands for the problem is solved, and 1 means the opposite, where would you put it today?
Parent(s) _____
Student _____
Teacher _____

What has helped to get it to that number on the scale?
Parent(s) _____
Student _____
Teacher _____

What will it look like when it moves up one notch on the scale? What will everyone be doing to help this happen?
Parent(s) _____
Student _____
Teacher _____

This worksheet is designed to help you remember the key points of a solution-focused meeting. It should not be rigidly followed. For example, a parent or student may first need to vent and to feel understood. After listening to them, you can gently shift the direction of the conversation to exceptions or goal setting.

Be persistent in solution-focused questioning. Typically, students or parents will answer from the problem picture, "This won't be happening." You need to persistently help them describe the solution picture by asking, "What will be happening instead?" If you still don't make any progress, you may need to go back to their concerns and re-clarify their goals for the meeting.

6. Scaling Questions

Students like scaling questions because they help to break a problem down into small pieces. The problem is not so overwhelming when they look at it on a scale. Scaling questions are visual and concrete tools that help students and teachers set realistic goals. With younger children, use something visual to highlight progress such as continuum of sad to happy faces, or a ladder that shows their progress. Scaling questions are ideal for setting goals in a student's Individual Personal Plan (IPP), in case conferences and in parent-teacher interviews.

You can use scaling questions in any situation. But, like any tool, they should be used with a purpose and not overused, or they will lose their effectiveness.

7. Solution-Focused Conflict Resolution

Teachers are often in the role of mediator in helping students solve interpersonal conflicts. When meeting with the students, you can use exception-finding, goal-setting or scaling questions to help shift to solution building:

When did the two of you get along? What helped then? **(exception-finding)**

Suppose things are better between the two of you, what will that look like? **(goal-setting)**

On a scale of 1 to 10, ten means that you are getting along, and one means the opposite, where would you put it today? Where would you like it to be on the scale? **(scaling goals)**

Many teachers are incorporating these questions in peer mediation programs, and the students use them when helping other students to solve problems. Other teachers are incorporating these questions in their curriculum for problem-solving skills. Table 11.4 gives some final tips for remaining solution-focused.

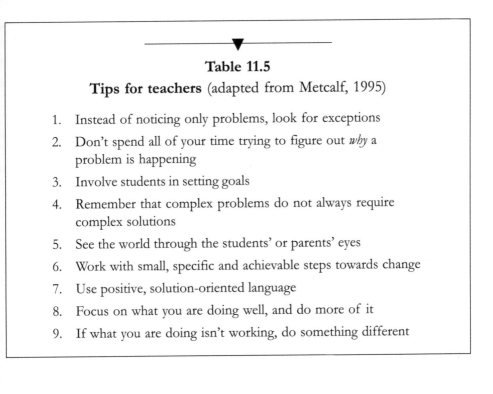

Table 11.5

Tips for teachers (adapted from Metcalf, 1995)

1. Instead of noticing only problems, look for exceptions
2. Don't spend all of your time trying to figure out *why* a problem is happening
3. Involve students in setting goals
4. Remember that complex problems do not always require complex solutions
5. See the world through the students' or parents' eyes
6. Work with small, specific and achievable steps towards change
7. Use positive, solution-oriented language
8. Focus on what you are doing well, and do more of it
9. If what you are doing isn't working, do something different

TWELVE

Solution-Focused Groups

Students are experts on what works for them and can share their expertise with others.

Workshop participants ask if the solution-focused model can be used in groups. Of course, the answer is affirmative because the model is a way of thinking and not simply a technique. When you integrate the solution-focused paradigm, the only limitation to its use is your imagination. As I became more skilled, I began to use the model in a variety of contexts.

Types of Solution-Focused Groups

THIS CHAPTER OUTLINES HOW TO ADAPT THE solution-focused model to working with groups and how it has been used in:

1. Counselling groups for children and adolescents
2. Parenting groups

3. Groups for school problems
4. Anger management groups
5. An alternative program for aggressive youth

Solution-focused groups are conducted using the same process used for individual or family meetings. Solution-focused questions are used to clarify the group's goals, and to highlight strengths and resources. Solution-focused tasks are given at the end of each group session.

Table 12.1 presents useful guidelines for conducting solution-focused counselling groups. As you read on, notice how these guidelines have been applied in many creative ways in different group settings.

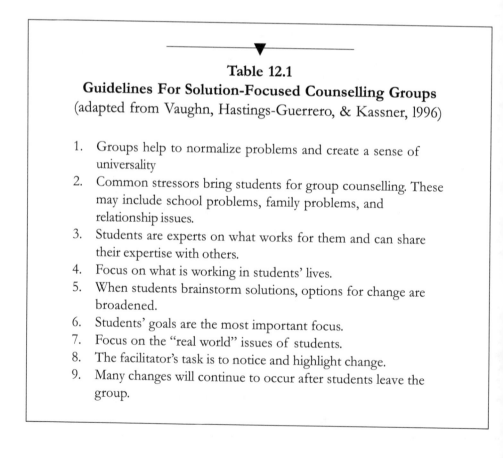

Table 12.1
Guidelines For Solution-Focused Counselling Groups
(adapted from Vaughn, Hastings-Guerrero, & Kassner, 1996)

1. Groups help to normalize problems and create a sense of universality
2. Common stressors bring students for group counselling. These may include school problems, family problems, and relationship issues.
3. Students are experts on what works for them and can share their expertise with others.
4. Focus on what is working in students' lives.
5. When students brainstorm solutions, options for change are broadened.
6. Students' goals are the most important focus.
7. Focus on the "real world" issues of students.
8. The facilitator's task is to notice and highlight change.
9. Many changes will continue to occur after students leave the group.

Solution-Focused Counselling Groups for Children and Adolescents

Traditionally, students have been grouped according to the problems they are struggling with. For example, children of divorce, children of alcoholic parents, or children suffering from the effects of abuse, are usually put in separate groups. Grouping students in this way can have a stigmatizing effect on the students and how others perceive them.

LaFountain and her colleagues set up a counselling group that focused on change rather than specific issues (1995). They set up a multi-grade, multi-age group for nine students, male and female, from grades six through eight. It is important to group students according to their developmental stages. A counsellor held an individual pre-screening meeting with each student to assess the appropriateness of the student for the group and whether the student wanted to be part of the group.

Students accepted into the group had a variety of concerns. For example, Andrew was worried about his alcoholic brother. Casey had persistent troublesome flashbacks about his brother who shot himself. The students' common goal was the desire to change something in their lives.

In the first group session, the counsellor asked the students to set some goals for themselves. "What is it you would like to change?" Casey stated, " I would like to change my memories…I get flashbacks, and I want to change it because it scares me" (Lafountain et al., p.44). Andrew's goal was to have a better relationship with his brother.

At the end of each group session, the children were given compliments and a task. Casey was asked to: "Keep track of when you are not having these scary memories of your brother. What are you doing?" He discovered that by keeping busy, and thinking of the good times with his brother, the flashbacks were not as frequent. Many of the children made progress with their goals and began to clarify what they could control in their lives and what they could not. Andrew realized that he could not change his substance-abusing brother. He decided, "to think about good stuff and what I want to do, instead of thinking about my brother" (p.46).

A total of four group sessions were held with the students. In the last session, the group discussion focused on how the students could keep change going and how to deal with setbacks. One of the greatest benefits of a solution-focused group is that it is a time-effective way of helping a number of students with diverse needs. The multi-age and multi-grade groupings allowed for more flexibility in scheduling and setting up the group.

Solution-Oriented Parenting Groups

Matthew Selekman (1991, 1993) describes how he set up solution-oriented parenting groups. The group was originally developed to help parents of adolescent substance abusers. Many of these parents had been involved in outpatient and inpatient treatment programs for their teens. The parents felt powerless. They didn't know how to deal with their teen's problems and expressed a need for more "hands on" parenting tools. Many of the teens refused to attend further therapy, so Selekman decided to work with the parents.

Referrals were obtained from churches, Tough Love, Families Anonymous, probation officers and schools. Selekman did not insist that both parents attend the group. Although the attendance of both parents would have been ideal, he worked with the parent most motivated to do something. He recommends keeping the groups homogeneous in terms of the age ranges of the adolescents. For example, parents of adolescents ranging from ages 12 to 15 should have a group separate from parents with older adolescents.

However, the groups were not homogeneous in terms of the parents' concerns. Parents whose teens were having school problems were in the same group with parents whose teens were abusing drugs. Group leaders found that this mix promoted more sharing and diversity in the group.

The group was limited to eight parents and was a closed group that ran for six sessions. Time intervals between sessions two through six were increased, to give parents time to practice the new concepts and to convey confidence in the parents' abilities.

When possible, Selekman works with a female co-therapist so that they can role-play parents' typical problem situations. One of them acts as the teen and the other acts as the parent. The group then discusses how to handle the situation differently.

The leaders actively reframe problems, highlight exceptions, normalize issues, and do a great deal of validation. They also share stories of how other parents have handled certain situations. The six sessions (1993, p.163) were organized according to the following topics:

1. Solution-oriented parenting:
   A new way of viewing and doing
2. Going for small changes
3. If it works, do more of it
4. If it doesn't work, do something different
5. Keeping change happening
6. Celebrating change.

In the first session, the group leaders took time to connect with the parents and allow parents to talk about their problems. They asked about the strengths and skills of each parent in the workplace or at home. These strengths were later utilized in the group discussions. For example, a father who was a supervisor took pride in how he handled "difficult employees." The group leaders later asked him how he would handle problems with his son as if he were a difficult employee, and the father changed his approach. Parents were also asked to talk about the strengths and resources of their adolescents.

During the group sessions, the leaders gave information about parenting, developmental stages of teens, and research regarding healthy families. For example, research about oppositional children, shows that: 1) ignoring or withdrawing from the emotional field can be very effective; and 2) excessively prolonged punishment just fosters rebellion and resentment (Selekman, 1991).

At the end of each group session, the parents were given compliments and homework tasks. In the last session, the parents were encouraged to talk about what they learned, how to maintain the changes they made, and how they will deal with anticipated setbacks. Parents, who felt that they had not made sufficient progress, were offered further family therapy.

Many of the adolescents were so pleased with the changes in their parents that they asked to meet with Selekman! After the group was finished, some parents formed a support group. Others agreed to act as "alumni" and be available as consultants to other parenting groups.

Selekman believes that solution-focused parenting groups can serve as a useful secondary prevention treatment program and can offer parents of substance abusers an alternative to more traditional 12-step programs. Finally, he argues that solution-focused groups are cost-effective and can help reduce agencies' wait lists.

Solution-Focused Groups for School Problems

Linda Metcalf (1995) has great ideas on how to set up solution-focused groups for children and adolescents. Groups can be set up under positive names such as "The Anger Managers," "The Homework Hustlers," and "Between Family and Friends."

A group of adolescent girls, who were having difficulties with their mothers, wanted to call their group the "I Hate My Mother" group (Metcalf, 1995, p.163). The group leader commented that they already had plenty of experience hating their mothers. He suggested that the group was going to be a place where they could learn to like or at least make peace with their mothers. They renamed the group "To Her with Love."

Table 12.2 offers practical suggestions for facilitating solution-focused groups (adapted from Metcalf, 1995).

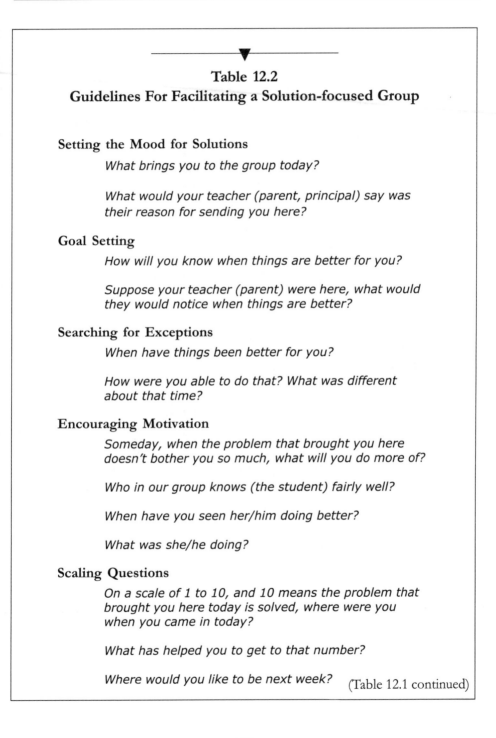

Table 12.2
Guidelines For Facilitating a Solution-focused Group

Setting the Mood for Solutions

What brings you to the group today?

What would your teacher (parent, principal) say was their reason for sending you here?

Goal Setting

How will you know when things are better for you?

Suppose your teacher (parent) were here, what would they would notice when things are better?

Searching for Exceptions

When have things been better for you?

How were you able to do that? What was different about that time?

Encouraging Motivation

Someday, when the problem that brought you here doesn't bother you so much, what will you do more of?

Who in our group knows (the student) fairly well?

When have you seen her/him doing better?

What was she/he doing?

Scaling Questions

On a scale of 1 to 10, and 10 means the problem that brought you here today is solved, where were you when you came in today?

What has helped you to get to that number?

Where would you like to be next week? (Table 12.1 continued)

Task Development

> *You have all told me great ideas about times when the problem doesn't bother you as much. Let's talk about what you might do in the next week to help you to stay on track.*

> *In the next week, I'd like you to keep track of when the problem doesn't bother you as much.*

Later Sessions

> *What's been going better this week? How have you done that?*

> *If I asked your teacher (parent), what do you think they would say?*

Anger Management Groups

Another useful technique, when working individually or with anger management groups, is to *externalize* the problem (White, 1989). The problem is discussed as if it is an entity or person that is separate from the student. For example, children who have temper problems are asked how they can stand up to "the temper monster." Children who have problems with theft are helped to fight against the influence of "sticky fingers."

Table 12.3 gives guidelines for how to use externalizing questions in the group setting (adapted from Metcalf, 1995, p.163).

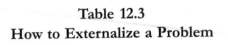

Table 12.3
How to Externalize a Problem

Goal Description

The student describes how life will be when the influence of the problem is lessened.

> *What will your life look like without the problem? (who will be doing what)*
>
> *If you could write a story or play, and title it Chapter Two, and the problem is gone, what would be different in your life?*
>
> *How would it be different from Chapter One?*

Problem Maintenance

The student thinks about how the problem is kept alive by her/his behaviour.

> *How have you allowed the problem to take over your life?*
>
> *What are you doing that allows it to keep coming back?*
>
> *How does the problem trick you into doing things that get you into trouble or doing things you dislike?*

Problem Externalization

The student pictures the problem as outside of her or himself.

> *If you could picture the problem, what would it look like?*
>
> *If you could give it a name, what would you name it?*

(Table 12.3 continued)

Competency/Exception Discovery

The student is asked to think about times when the problem's influence isn't as intense or doesn't affect the student's life.

There must be times when the problem doesn't stand a chance even though it tries to bother you. How do you stop it?

Suppose the other group members could see you putting the problem in its place, what would they see you doing?

Task Development for Competencies

The student is asked to do more of what lessened the problem's influence in her/his life.

From your description in the Chapter 2 story, what are some things you could do gradually to avoid the problem?

What would the audience applaud you doing when they watch you in Chapter Two?

Where would you like to be tomorrow? Next week?

What is your plan today, based on the steps you listed when anger doesn't take control? Keep track of what helps to keep anger in its place.

The externalization technique is extremely useful when helping students deal with anger management problems (Metcalf, 1995). It helps students to let go of things that bother them. Give them the following questions to help focus on times when they let anger take over and times when they controlled their anger successfully:

Situations when I let anger take over...

Situations when I don't let anger take over...

Scaling questions can be used to externalize anger. Notice that 10 usually stands for times when the student is in charge of the problem and 1 means simply the opposite. Again, this use of language orients the student towards success:

> *On a scale of 1 to 10, 10 stands for you are in charge of anger, and 1 means that anger is in charge of you, where are you today?*
>
> *How did you get to that number on the scale? What helped?*
>
> *What will it look like when you move up one notch on the scale? What would your teacher (parents, friends) say?*

An Alternative to Suspension Program

One school division created a solution-based program for students who were suspended for serious aggressive acts (Cooper, 1998). School professionals were concerned about the growing number of long-term suspensions and many believed that suspensions only served to shift problems from the schools to the streets. They wanted a program that protected both the school and victims of school violence, and one that also addressed the social/emotional needs of the perpetrators.

An "Alternative to Suspension Program" was created. Students referred to the program had a history of suspensions and were seen as a risk to others or themselves. Many had problems other than school problems, such as legal and family difficulties.

Student attendance of the program was completely voluntary. When students first visited the program, they were told that the staff had little information about them and none was wanted at that point. They were told that the prime concern was "the student's future, not his past."

The students established their own goals and were responsible for meeting these goals. When they didn't appear to be meeting their stated goals, no consequences were set. Rather, staff took an "I'm confused" stance and asked the students to explain how what they are doing or not doing, was helping them reach their goals. Staff and students discussed strategies that would help the students deal with their legal, family and school problems.

Epilogue

In this book, I have outlined the solution-focused model and its usefulness in working with school problems. The solution-focused model is a way of thinking, and not simply a set of questions or techniques to memorize. Many workshop participants tell me that adopting the solution-focused approach has benefited their personal as well as their professional lives.

The solution-focused model is respectful, positive, and builds on the assumption that students and parents have resources and strengths. When we work from a stance of positive expectancy, it transforms our work and our daily interactions. Many professionals tell me the model has positively affected them and their work environment. Indeed, I am convinced that the solution-focused model helps to reduce staff burnout.

This book has discussed how to work with "difficult" students and parents. Let us remember that problem behaviour is better understood when it is viewed within its context. Many "difficult" parents are overworked and overwhelmed. Some have their own unhappy memories about school. Others may be struggling with financial problems, emotional problems, or mental health issues. Similarly, "difficult" students may be struggling with family difficulties, poverty, and peer relationships. The solution-focused model offers you tools to enhance students' resiliency and strategies for working with difficult problems.

As I wrote this book, I thought of all the questions that I hadn't answered. Inevitably, no book can be all encompassing. I am working on a second book and also plan on developing audiotapes and videotapes to help you to learn this model. Please send me your suggestions for topics and resources that would be useful to you.

I would like to encourage you to start using the solution-focused model right away. You will be pleasantly surprised at the difference it will make in your work.

Nancy McConkey

Mailing List

Do You Have a Success Story?

Send me your story of how you used the solution-focused model and it may be included in my next book. Send a brief overview by e-mail to soltalk @telusplanet.net, or by mail to Solution Talk, P.O. Box 247b, Bragg Creek, Alberta, Canada, T0L 0K0. Your work will be fully credited.

Future Resources and Workshops

We are developing a line of audiotapes, videotapes and workbooks to compliment this book and our solution-focused workshops. If you want more information about these future resources, be sure to get on our mailing list. I would appreciate hearing your suggestions for topics and resources that would be useful to you.

Workshops and Keynotes

To book the author for workshops or conferences, call us at (403) 216-8255 or see the author's schedule at www.solutiontalk.ab.ca

Yes, Put Me on Your Mailing List for Future Resources

Name: _____

Title/Role: _____

Agency/School: _____

Address: _____

City: _____

Province/State: _____

Country: _____ Postal Code/Zip: _____

Phone: (____) _____ Fax: (____) _____

E-mail: _____
(We respect your privacy. We do not rent, exchange or sell our mailing list.)

Resources/Books/Topics/Workshops I am interested in are:

_____

_____

_____

_____

Keynotes and Workshops Available from Solution Talk

Solving School Problems: Solution-Focused Strategies

"In 27 years of teaching, this is one of the most useful workshops I have attended."
Barry Pratte, Teacher

This workshop is for a wide range of professionals who work with school problems. Teachers, principals, counsellors and resource personnel will learn how to:

- Work with difficult parents and students
- Utilize brief, positive interventions in the classroom
- Conduct solution-focused parent/teacher meetings
- Negotiate achievable, realistic goals with parents and students
- Shift from problems to solutions

Solution-Focused Strategies for Nurses and Health Care Professionals

"Thanks for a great workshop!"
Carol Bassingthwaighte, RN

This workshop shows how nurses, dieticians, physiotherapists, occupational therapists, health care educators and other health care professionals can:

- Motivate patients
- Use solution-focused language to create hope
- Help family members deal with illness
- Deal with non-compliant patients
- Help patients cope with chronic illness

Level 1: Solution-Focused Counselling

"I don't think you can go back to problem-oriented thinking once you have taken this course. This workshop accelerates the creation of new ideas and helps me work with very difficult situations."
Paul Bohn, Family Support Worker

This workshop will help any human service or school professional who wants to be more effective in working with clients and students. You will learn how to:

- Do single session counselling
- Reduce defensiveness and blame
- Negotiate concrete, solvable goals
- Develop brief, positive interventions
- Use solution-focused questions to move from problems to solutions

Level 2: Working with Difficult Clients

"Nancy, you are a high-energy, excellent presenter. You have inspired me to incorporate this model in my practice."
Esther Oga, Counsellor

This workshop is for counsellors who are familiar with the solution-focused approach and who want to increase their confidence and expertise in using the model. Develop confidence in how to:

- Design solution-focused homework tasks
- Deal with setbacks
- Work with involuntary clients
- Address issues of suicide and violence
- Work with the long-term and challenging clients

Working with Child Protection Clients

"I loved the workshop. I found it to be one of the most energizing, useful workshops that I have attended."
Tammy Holt, Child Protection Worker

This workshop is for supervisors, child protection workers, and other professionals who work with child protection clients. You will learn how to:

- Defuse resistance
- Engage clients with the use of solution-focused language
- Use solution-focused strategies when abuse is denied or minimized
- Assess for "signs of safety" as well as for "signs of risk"
- Negotiate achievable treatment plans

Working with Substance Abuse Problems

"This presenter really knows her stuff! The workshop was awesome!"
Mike Williams, Addictions Counsellor

The solution-focused approach is very effective for helping clients with addiction problems and it can be utilized in both inpatient and outpatient programs. Learn how to:

- Apply this model to a wide range of addiction problems
- Build client motivation to change
- Listen for clients' hidden motivators for change
- Deal with involuntary clients
- Deal with multiple problems

Working with Involuntary Clients

"This was by far the BEST workshop I have attended. Nancy was a resource that I could have cornered for many, many hours and I continued to be impressed with what she had to say."
Ann Wandler, Counsellor

Do you work with clients, who say, "I was sent here but I don't want to be here"? If this sounds familiar, this workshop will be useful to you! Learn how to:

- Defuse client resistance
- Enhance motivation
- Listen for the "hidden customer"
- Negotiate achievable treatment goals with the referral source

Working with Couples and Families

"I've just recently returned from my workshop with you. I want to tell you how rejuvenated and energized I felt with the strategies you presented. Days later I'm still feeling that way."
Natalie Handy, Counsellor

Involving family members is one of the most significant things you can do to enhance treatment success. Even when family members are not physically present, you can involve them in the interview with the skillful use of questions. Learn how to:

- Do family counselling with one person
- Conduct solution-focused family and couple sessions
- Take charge of the interview
- Interrupt destructive patterns
- Involve children and youth

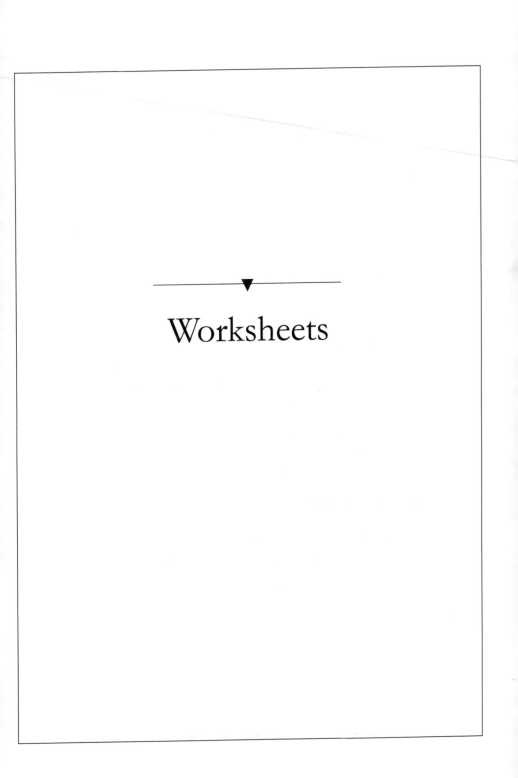

Worksheets

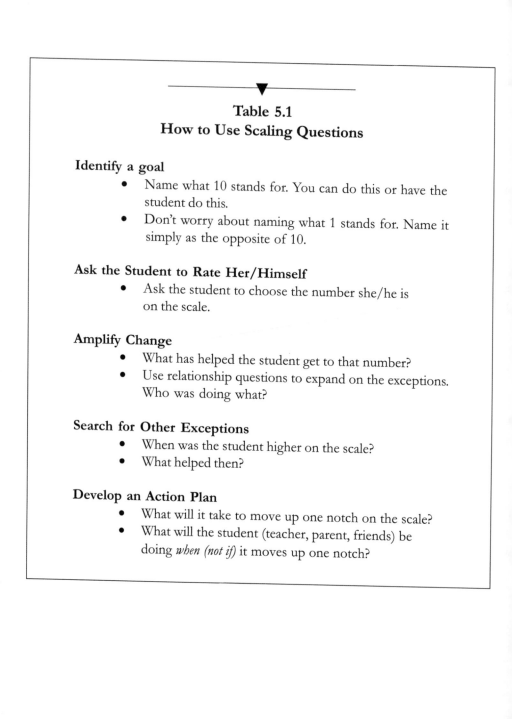

Table 5.1
How to Use Scaling Questions

Identify a goal
- Name what 10 stands for. You can do this or have the student do this.
- Don't worry about naming what 1 stands for. Name it simply as the opposite of 10.

Ask the Student to Rate Her/Himself
- Ask the student to choose the number she/he is on the scale.

Amplify Change
- What has helped the student get to that number?
- Use relationship questions to expand on the exceptions. Who was doing what?

Search for Other Exceptions
- When was the student higher on the scale?
- What helped then?

Develop an Action Plan
- What will it take to move up one notch on the scale?
- What will the student (teacher, parent, friends) be doing *when (not if)* it moves up one notch?

Table 6.1
Framework for a Solution-Focused Meeting

The Meeting

- Establish rapport
- Obtain the student's perception of the problem
- Establish the purpose of the meeting
- Explore the solution picture
- Explore exceptions
- Normalize and validate throughout the meeting
- Scaling questions

Think Break

- Formulate feedback for the student

Feedback to the Student

- Compliments
- Bridging statement
- Solution-focused homework task

Table 6.2
Solution-Focused Meeting Worksheet

Name: _____ Date: _____ Meeting # _____

Type of Meeting: (individual, parent/child, teacher/student) _____

Family Members Present: _____

Others Present in the Meeting: _____

Other Involved Professionals: (ie. teacher aid, pediatrician, probation officer)
_____

1. Current Problem(s): parent, student and teacher's views of the problem
_____

2. Relevant History (ie. medication, learning disabilities, etc.)
_____

3. Solution Picture: Parent, student and teacher's views
_____

4. Exceptions (when are things a little better)
_____

5. Scaling Questions
   Motivation: _____
   Confidence: _____
   Progress: _____

6. Feedback to the Student/Parent
   Compliments _____
   Bridging Statement _____
   Task _____

7. Plans for the Next Meeting _____

▼

Table 8.2
Pre-Interview Worksheet

How will you know this meeting has been helpful? What will be different after we meet?

Tell me when things were better for you.

On a scale of 1 to 10, with 10 meaning things are as good as they will be in your life, and 1 means the opposite, where would you put yourself on the scale today?
(worse) 1 ....10 (as good as possible)

What has helped you get to that number on the scale? (no matter what number you pick)
What have you been doing? What have others been doing?

How will you be able to tell when it has moved up one notch? What would be different about you? About other people in your life (parents, teachers, friends)?

Table 9.2
Solution-Focused Parent Referral Sheet

Dear Parent(s), thank you for taking the time to complete this sheet. It will help me to help your child.

Name of Student _____ Grade _____ Date _____

Your Name _____ Phone No. (H)_____ (W) _____

Your Relationship to the Student _____

1. What are your concerns? _____

_____

2. What have you tried so far? What has helped? _____

_____

3. What are your child's strengths, hobbies, and interests? What motivates her/him?

_____

4. When have things been better? (small things or times when things are a little better) _____

_____

5. On a scale of 1 to10, and 10 means that your child is doing as best as possible, and 1 means the opposite, what number is it today? _____

6. How will you know it has moved up one notch on the scale? What will your child be doing? What else will help? _____

_____

_____
Parent Signature

Table 9.3
Solution-Focused Teacher Referral Form

Dear Colleague, thank you for taking the time to complete this sheet. It will help me when I meet with the student.

Name of Student _____ Grade _____ Date _____

Your Name _____ School _____

Phone _____

1. What are your concerns? _____

_____

2. What have you tried so far? What has helped a little? _____

_____

3. Please list the times when you notice the student is doing well. This will give us clues to solutions. Please be as specific as possible. For example, "She focused on her work for 10 minutes and tuned out the other students." "He kept his temper in check." _____

_____

_____

4. On a scale of 1 to 10, and 10 means the student is doing as best as possible, and 1 means the opposite, what number would you give the student? _____

5. How will you know when the student has moved up one notch on the scale? What will the student be doing? What else will help? _____

_____

_____
Teacher Signature

▼

Table 11.4
Solution-Focused Worksheet for
Parent-Teacher Meetings

Student Name _____ Parent's names _____ Date _____

Number of Meetings _____ Present at the Meeting _____

Why are we here? What are our concerns? What is the problem?
Parent(s) _____
Student _____
Teacher _____

When has the student been doing better?
Parent(s) _____
Student _____
Teacher _____

Suppose the problems that brought us to this meeting are solved, what will that look like?
Parent(s) _____
Student _____
Teacher _____

On a scale of 1 to 10, and 10 stands for the problem is solved, and 1 means the opposite, where would you put it today?
Parent(s) _____
Student _____
Teacher _____

What has helped to get it to that number on the scale?
Parent(s) _____
Student _____
Teacher _____

What will it look like when it moves up one notch on the scale? What will everyone be doing to help this happen?
Parent(s) _____
Student _____
Teacher _____

Index of Case Examples

		more engaged in the interview when the counsellor first tries to understand his situation by exploring how drugs are helpful to him. Later, he is more willing to explore how they are not helpful.
I want you to see my daughter for counselling right away!	64	A mother begins to see changes in her daughter because she believes the daughter has seen the counsellor. A positive expectancy for change creates change.
She hides under her desk	65	A grade two student hides under her desk when she is upset. Solution-focused questions help the teacher shift from a negative to a positive view of the student's behaviour.
He's a hero in his own life	67	A grade nine student is in danger of failing his drafting class, and his girlfriend has just had a baby. After the teacher begins to focus on exceptions, he recognizes that his student has potential.
I don't think it will change	79	An adolescent isn't very optimistic that counselling will help her family. Scaling questions help to draw out her ideas about what will help.
We haven't dealt with grandma's death	82	Initially, a 17-year-old girl is angry and uncooperative in counselling. Scaling questions help to reveal her hidden concerns about her family.
A reading problem	85	A grade five teacher is frustrated with a student and his parents. She believes they don't recognize the seriousness of his reading problem. Scaling questions, used in

		a parent-teacher interview, quickly lead to solutions.
I'm on probation	89	A student, who is on probation, is transferred to a new school and does not appear very motivated to change. The principal skillfully uses solution-focused questions to engage the student in setting goals for the school year.
I almost killed my-self this week	95	A client is suicidal. Exception-finding questions help to build motivation and hope. Scaling questions are used to assess suicide risk and to work towards signs of safety.
I want to get my wacky self back	101	A teenager describes her solution picture in terms of getting her "wacky" self back – an indication to her of improved happiness and self-esteem. The importance of using the student's language when exploring for solutions is demonstrated.
The lockers would all be the same colour.	104	An elementary student has fetal alcohol syndrome. When asked a simple future-oriented question, he describes solutions that will help him to cope.
I don't want to be here	105	A student is sent, against his wishes, for counselling. Validation and normalization help to reduce the student's defensiveness.
Fighting the temper monster	114	A nine-year-old girl has problems with physical aggression at school and at home. This case example shows how to use the externalization technique to deal with temper problems. A transcript of the first session highlights key solution-focused interventions.

Pretend to be a good student	134	A grade 10 student skips school and is on the verge of failing school. She copes by pretending to be interested in school. Her unique solution is used to build solutions.
I don't have a dope problem	146	A teacher refers a high school student to the counsellor because she believes the student uses marijuana in school. The student is adamant that he doesn't have a problem. This case shows how to work with a student who is an involuntary client, and how to listen for the "hidden customer."
The teacher is a jerk	153	A student blames the teacher for his problems – initially, he is not willing to take responsibility for change. This case example shows how to work with resistant students, and how to shift the student from a complainant to a customer relationship.
Do something with these students!	167	A grade two teacher has sent two students to the principal's office for misbehaviour. This case demonstrates how principals can conduct solution-focused discipline.
A ten percent average	172	At the end of her first semester in grade eight, a student's average was only ten percent. She is transferred to a new school for the second semester. The principal skillfully uses solution-focused questions to help her make a fresh start.
Help us come together as a team	177	A school staff group is split into two camps regarding how to handle discipline problems in their school. Solution-focused questions are used to team-build.

Parents who refused to attend parent-teacher interviews	188	Teachers are frustrated with "problem" parents who refuse to attend meetings regarding their child's school problems. The teachers realize that all of their contact with these parents is problem-focused. They begin to focus on exceptions and a more cooperative relationship develops.
The solution-focused classroom	190	A teacher uses the solution-focused model to involve students in generating guidelines for appropriate behaviour. Students are more likely to follow through when they are involved in the goal-setting process.

Concept Index

O'Hanlon, W., 9, 10, 11, 24, 127

P

Paradigm, 5, 15, 140
Parent referral worksheet, 162
Parenting groups, solution-focused,
    200-202
Parent-teacher meetings,
    how to shift from problem
    talk to solution talk, 49, 102
    solution-focused worksheet,
Peller, J, 144
Positive reframing, 186-188
Positive expectancy, importance
    of, 23, 33-35
Pretend tasks with young children, 135
Pre-treatment change, 63-64
    case example, 64
    usefulness in schools, 27
    worksheet, 131, 223
Principals, solution-focused strategies
for, 165-183
    discipline meetings, 46, 166-171
    case example, 167
    transfer of problem students, 172
    working with staff, 177-183
Positive reframing, 186
Positive expectancy, importance
    of, 23, 33-35
Problem patterns, 19
Problem-saturated thinking, 19, 28
Problem-solving models,
    traditional assumptions of, 10
    problem-focused questions
    versus solution-focused
    questions, 12
Problem talk, how to shift from, 41-57

Q

Questions as interventions,

types of questions, 12-13
    reportive, 12-13
    constructive, 12-13
Quick interview, 92

R

Rapport building, 37, 101, 105
Reading problem, 85
Referring person, 160
Reframing, 186-188
Referral worksheets,
    Parent, 162, 224
    Teacher, 163, 225
Reportive questions, 12-13
Research,
    effectiveness of single session
    counselling, 32
    effect of counsellors' beliefs on
    counselling outcomes, 23
    on resiliency, 69-72
    pre-treatment change, 25
    effect of positive expectancy,
    23, 33-35
    teachers' beliefs as significant
    determinant on students' IQ
    tests, 23
Relationships, types of therapeutic
relationships,
    visitor-type, 56-57
    complainant-type, 56
    customer-type, 55
Reportive questions, 12-13
Resiliency, 69-72
    how to enhance student
    resiliency, 71-72
    profile of a resilient child,
    internal and external factors, 71-72
    research, 69-72
Rosenthal, H., 23, 35

Tips for teachers, 196
Tomm, K., 18

U
Understanding the student's
situation, 37

V
Visitor-type relationship, 56
Validation, importance of, 37, 105
    case example, 105
Vaughn, K., 198

W
Walter, J., 144
Weiner-Davis, M., 10, 11, 24, 25, 127
White, M., 19, 28
Worksheets, 219
    parent-teacher meeting, 193, 226
    pre-interview worksheet, 131, 222
    scaling questions, 76, 220
    solution-focused meeting, 100, 111,
    221, 222
    solution-focused parent referral
    form, 162, 224
    solution-focused teacher-
    referral form, 163, 225

References

Ah Shene, D. (1999). Resiliency: A vision of hope. *Developments,* 18 (7), Alberta Alcohol and Addictions Council.

Berg, I. K. & Miller, S. D. (1992). *Working with the problem drinker: A solution-focused approach.* New York: W.W. Norton.

Berg, I. (1994). *Family based services: A solution-focused approach.* New York: W.W. Norton

Cooper, J. L., (1998). An alternative solution to school violence. *Journal of Systemic Therapies,* 17 (3), 12-23.

De Jong, P. & Berg, I. K. (1998). *Interviewing for solutions.* Pacific Grove, CA: Brooks/Cole Publishing Company

de Shazer, S. (1985). *Keys to solution in brief therapy.* New York: W.W. Norton.

de Shazer, S. (1988). *Clues: Investigating solutions in brief therapy.* New York: W.W. Norton.

de Shazer, S. (April 27-28, 1989). *Solution-focused therapy.* Workshop, Grande Prairie.

de Shazer, S., Berg, I. K., Lipchik, E., Nunnally, E., Molnar, A., Gingerich, W., & Weiner-Davis, M. (1986). Brief therapy: Focused solution development. *Family Process,* 25, 207-221.

Dolan, Y.M. (1991). *Resolving sexual abuse. Solution-focused therapy and Ericksonian hypnosis for adult survivors.* New York: W.W. Norton.

Durrant, M. (1993). *Residential treatment: A cooperative, competency-based approach to therapy and program design.* New York: W.W. Norton and Company.

Durant, M. (1995). *Creative strategies for school problems. Solutions for psychologists and teachers.* New York: W.W. Norton

Kral, R. (1994). *Solution-focused methods for school problems.* (Cassette recording). Milwaukee: A Brief Family Therapy Center AudioTape

La Fountain, R., Garner, N., & Boldosser, S. (1995). Solution-focused counselling groups for children and adolescents. *Journal of Systemic Therapies,* 14 (4), 39-51.

Lipchik, E. & de Shazer, S. (1986). *The purposeful interview. Journal of Strategic and Systemic Therapies,* 5, (1, 2), 88-99.

McConkey, N. (1997). Single session counselling. Making the most of your only session with a client. *The Social Worker,* 65 (1), 1-5.

McConkey, N. (1998). A brief solution-focused approach to solving school problems. *Journal of Guidance and Counselling,* 13 (3), 19-22.

McFarland, B. (1995). Brief therapy and eating disorders. A practical guide to solution-focused work with clients. San Francisco: Jossey-Bass Inc

Metcalf, L. (1995). *Counseling toward solutions. A practical, solution-focused program for working with students, teachers & parents.* New York: The Center for Applied Research in Education.

Metcalf, L. (1998). *Solution-focused group therapy.* New York: The Free Press.

Metcalf, L. (1999). *Teaching toward solutions. Step-by-step strategies for handling academic, behavior and family issues in the classroom.* New York: Prentice Hall.

Molnar, A. & Lindquist, B. (1989). *Changing Problem Behavior in Schools*. San Francisco: Jossey-Bass.

Osenton, T. & Chang, J., (1999). Solution-oriented classroom management: A proactive application with young children. *Journal of Systemic Therapies*, <u>18</u>, (2), 65-75.

O'Hanlon, W. H. & Weiner-Davis, M. (1989). *In search of solutions. A new direction in psychotherapy*. New York: W.W. Norton & Company.

Rosenthal, H. & Jacobson, L. (1968). *Pygmalion in the classroom*. New York: Holt, Rinehart, and Winston.

Rowan, T., & O'Hanlon, W. H. (1999). *Solution-oriented therapy for chronic and severe mental illness*. Toronto: John Wiley & Sons.

Schlechty, P. (1990). *Schools for the 21st century*. San Francisco: Jossey-Bass.

Selekman, M. (1991). The solution-oriented parenting group: A treatment alternative that works. *Journal of Strategic and Systemic Therapies*, <u>10</u> (1), 36-50.

Selekman, M. (1993). *Pathways to change: Brief therapy with difficult adolescents*. New York: Guilford Press.

Selekman, M. (1997). *Solution-focused therapy with children. Harnessing family strengths for systemic change*. New York: Guilford Press.

Slive, A., MacLaurin, B., Oaklander, M., & Amundson, J. (1996). Walk-in single sessions: A new paradigm in clinical service delivery. *Journal of Systemic Therapies*, <u>14</u> (1), 3-11.

Talmon, M. (1990). *Single session therapy. Maximizing the first (and often only) 0therapeutic encounter*. San Francisco: Jossey-Bass.

Tomm, K., (1985). Circular interviewing: A multifaceted clinical tool. In D. Campbell, & R. Draper (Eds.), *Applications of systemic family therapy: The Milan approach* (pp. 33-45). London: Grune & Stratton.

Vaugn, K., Hastings-Guerrero, S., & Kassner, C., (1996). Solution-oriented in-patient group therapy. *Journal of Systemic Therapies*, 15 (3), 1-13.

Walter, J. & Peller, J. (1992). *Becoming solution-focused in brief therapy.* New York: Brunner/Mazel.

Weiner-Davis, M., de Shazer, S. & Gingerich, W. (1987). Building on pretreatment change to construct the therapeutic solution: An exploratory study. *Journal of Marital and Family Therapy.* 13, 350-363.

White, M. (1989, Summer). The externalizing of the problem and the re-authoring of lives and relationships. Adelaide, South Australia: *Dulwich Centre Newsletter*, 3-21.

Order a Copy of this Book for your Library or a Friend

Order Form: Go to the order form on the back of this page.

Fax orders:

Send via fax 24 hours a day to (403) 949-4493. Institutions should fax valid purchase orders with contact information. Individuals must provide credit card information and signature.

Telephone orders:

Call Toll-Free 1-866-30-4TALK (8255) or (403) 216-TALK (8255).

On-line orders:

Go to www.solutiontalk.ab.ca to order on our secured website (credit cards only).

Postal orders:

Complete the order form and mail with your cheque or money order to Solution Talk Inc., P.O. Box 247b, Bragg Creek, Alberta, Canada, T0L 0K0. If you are paying by credit card, be sure to provide all of the requested information and your signature.

Special Quantity Discounts:

This book and other future products are available at quantity discounts. For more information, please contact us and tell us how the book will be used and the date it will be needed.

Order Form

Customer Information

Name: _____ Title: _____

Agency/School: _____

Address: _____

City: _____ Province/State: _____

Country: _____ Postal Code/Zip: _____

Telephone: (____) _____ Fax: (____) _____

E-mail: _____

We respect your privacy. We do not rent, exchange or sell our mailing list.

Please send me _____ copy/copies
Canadian orders $44.95 (CDN) each $ _____
United States orders $30.00 (US) each

Add Shipping:
Canadian orders $8 (CDN) for first book $ _____
($1.00 for each additional book)

United States orders $6.00 (US) for first book $ _____
($1.00 for each additional book)

Subtotal $ _____

Add 7% GST (Canadian residents only) $ _____

Total: $ _____

Payment:

Cheque or Money Order (payable to Solution Talk Inc.)

Credit card: Visa: _____ MasterCard: _____

Card Number: _____

Name on Card: _____ Expiry Date: _____

Authorized Signature: _____

Order a Copy of this Book for your Library or a Friend

Order Form: Go to the order form on the back of this page.

Fax orders:

Send via fax 24 hours a day to (403) 949-4493. Institutions should fax valid purchase orders with contact information. Individuals must provide credit card information and signature.

Telephone orders:

Call Toll-Free 1-866-30-4TALK (8255) or (403) 216-TALK (8255).

On-line orders:

Go to www.solutiontalk.ab.ca to order on our secured website (credit cards only).

Postal orders:

Complete the order form and mail with your cheque or money order to Solution Talk Inc., P.O. Box 247b, Bragg Creek, Alberta, Canada, T0L 0K0. If you are paying by credit card, be sure to provide all of the requested information and your signature.

Special Quantity Discounts:

This book and other future products are available at quantity discounts. For more information, please contact us and tell us how the book will be used and the date it will be needed.

Order Form

Customer Information

Name: _____ Title: _____

Agency/School: _____

Address: _____

City: _____ Province/State: _____

Country: _____ Postal Code/Zip: _____

Telephone: (____) _____ Fax: (____) _____

E-mail: _____

We respect your privacy. We do not rent, exchange or sell our mailing list.

Please send me _____ copy/copies
Canadian orders $44.95 (CDN) each $ _____
United States orders $30.00 (US) each

Add Shipping:

Canadian orders $8 (CDN) for first book $ _____
($1.00 for each additional book)

United States orders $6.00 (US) for first book $ _____
($1.00 for each additional book)

Subtotal $ _____

Add 7% GST (Canadian residents only) $ _____

Total: $ _____

Payment:

Cheque or Money Order (payable to Solution Talk Inc.)

Credit card: Visa: _____ MasterCard: _____

Card Number: _____

Name on Card: _____ Expiry Date: _____

Authorized Signature: _____

rder a Copy of this Book for our Library or a Friend

Order Form: Go to the order form on the back of this page.

Fax orders:

Send via fax 24 hours a day to (403) 949-4493. Institutions should fax valid purchase orders with contact information. Individuals must provide credit card information and signature.

Telephone orders:

Call Toll-Free 1-866-30-4TALK (8255) or (403) 216-TALK (8255).

On-line orders:

Go to www.solutiontalk.ab.ca to order on our secured website (credit cards only).

Postal orders:

Complete the order form and mail with your cheque or money order to Solution Talk Inc., P.O. Box 247b, Bragg Creek, Alberta, Canada, T0L 0K0. If you are paying by credit card, be sure to provide all of the requested information and your signature.

Special Quantity Discounts:

This book and other future products are available at quantity discounts. For more information, please contact us and tell us how the book will be used and the date it will be needed.

Order Form

Customer Information

Name: _____ Title: _____

Agency/School: _____

Address: _____
_____

City: _____ Province/State: _____

Country: _____ Postal Code/Zip: _____

Telephone: (____) _____ Fax: (____) _____

E-mail: _____

Please send me _____ copy/copies
Canadian orders $44.95 (CDN) each $ _____
United States orders $30.00 (US) each

Add Shipping:

Canadian orders $8 (CDN) for first book $ _____
($1.00 for each additional book)

United States orders $6.00 (US) for first book $ _____
($1.00 for each additional book)

Subtotal $ _____

Add 7% GST (Canadian residents only) $ _____

Total: $ _____

Payment:

Cheque or Money Order (payable to Solution Talk Inc.)

Credit card: Visa: _____ MasterCard: _____

Card Number: _____

Name on Card: _____ Expiry Date: _____

Authorized Signature: _____